Erica Wilson's
CHRISTMAS
WORLD

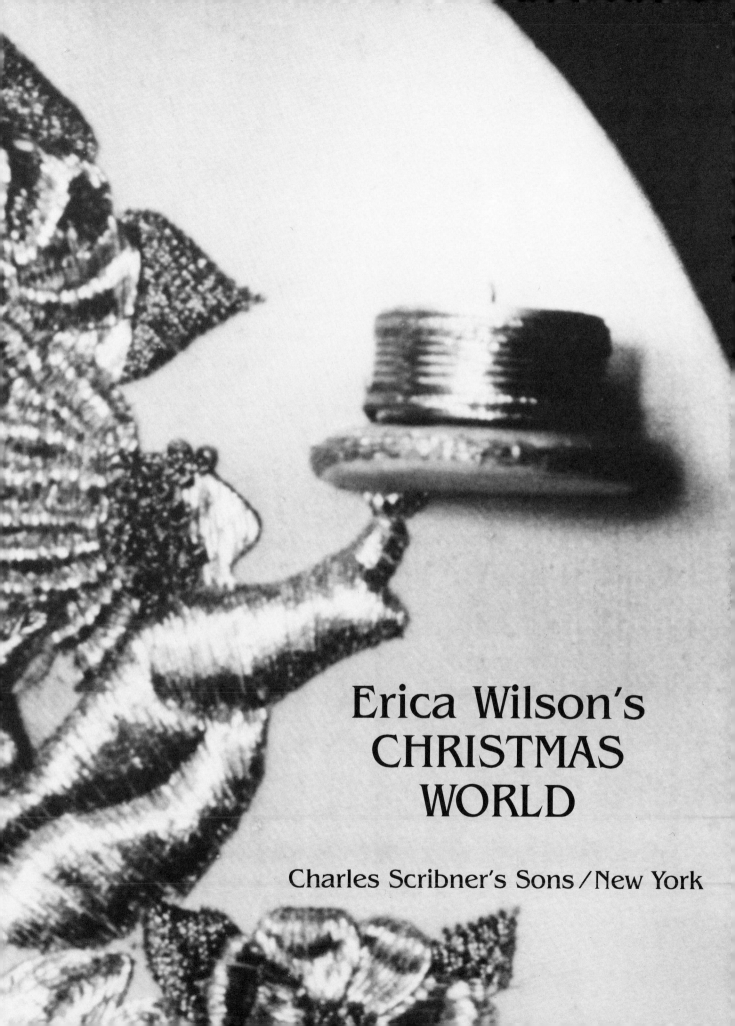

Erica Wilson's CHRISTMAS WORLD

Charles Scribner's Sons / New York

The Beatrix Potter designs interpreted in stitches by Erica appear by special permission of Frederick Warne & Co., Inc.

Chessie®, on pages 44 and 104 and stitched by Erica, is shown by special permission of the Chessie® System. Chessie® is the official symbol of the Chesapeake and Ohio Railway.

The following photographers contributed to the book: Saul Leiter, Shecter Lee, Leonard Nones, and Vladimir Kagan.

Library of Congress Cataloging in Publication Data

Wilson, Erica.
  Erica Wilson's Christmas world.

  1. Christmas decorations. 2. Handicraft.
I. Title.
TT900.C4W54   746.4   80-18446
ISBN 0-684-17651-3

1 3 5 7 9 11 13 15 17 19 Q/P 20 18 16 14 12 10 8 6 4 2

Printed in the United States of America

Book design by Viola Andrycich

CONTENTS

A family Christmas in Nantucket, with Erica, Vladimir,
and the children, Jessica, Illya, and Vanessa.

"**A** Merry Christmas to us all, my dears. God bless us!" — Bob Cratchit in "A Christmas Carol" by Charles Dickens

Making things for Christmas is really what Christmas is all about—the satisfaction of seeing the delight on someone's face when you say, "I made it especially for you," or discovering once again how proudly the Christmas angel you made last year stands atop the tree.

In this mass-production age, it is a joy to conjure up lovely Victorian scenes of the family decorating the tree in the parlor while the snow swirls outside. But our nostalgia for the past is more than an escape from an atmosphere of commercialism; it brings an awareness of and an appreciation for things made by hand. Once again, "homemade" means better than "store-bought."

Which is better? Christmas in the city, with its glittering lights and its shops filled with treasures, or Christmas in the country, with the crisp sparkling air and the smell of pine trees, wood smoke (once again, just like the old days!) rising from the chimney, and a roaring fire in the grate. Whichever Christmas it is, the most exciting part of it all is secretly putting the finishing touches to presents and decorations, some of which have been under hidden construction for months, or to others whipped up in minutes—those that have just seen the light of day (or night, depending on how secretly you've slaved to complete them). In this book you'll find designs that will be heirlooms and things that are ideal to do only moments before you need them (to liven up that special spot) or as the gift that no one but you can give.

There are three sections in the book. The first part, "O Tannenbaum!," shows how to make all sorts of things for the Christmas tree. The second part, "Deck the Halls," suggests decorations you can make for the house. The last part, "'Tis the Season to be Jolly," gives you ideas for gifts, as well as for things you can make for small members of the family—and things *they* can make, too.

FABRICS, COLORS, AND TEXTURES

Use this book as you would a recipe book. Find an idea you like, and collect the "ingredients" from the listing given with each design. As you make things, variations will suggest themselves to you, and it won't be long before you produce your own specialties, adding the individual touches that make it your own.

MATERIALS

Collect materials all year round like a squirrel. You'll find it so useful to have a basic collection ready to be used when the right idea comes along. Plastic canvas, needlepoint canvas, linen or cotton fabric for crewel work, patch-work fabrics, evenweave Aida cloth for cross stitching, cotton floss, wools, metal threads, ribbons, sequins, and beads can all be stored and waiting ready for just that right moment when inspiration comes.

PLASTIC CANVAS, small squares 3″ and 4″ Plastic canvas comes in several different varieties. It is an ideal material for Christmas ornaments because it is firm yet flexible and always looks neat and tailored. You can cut each piece to size and then join the finished pieces with a simple lacing stitch. The small squares are portable and can be used just like patchwork, but an added bonus is that the stiffness of this marvelous space-age material allows you to make things in three dimensions precisely and professionally.

INTERLOCKED CANVAS Interlocked canvas is woven in such a way that it does not ravel easily, making it also useful for three-dimensional projects, such as Santa in a Balloon on page 138 and for the openwork lace of the angel's wings on page 54.

AIDA CLOTH This is the fabric used for counted cross-stitch. It comes in different weaves and colors. When cross stitching is done finely in cotton floss, it has a lovely smooth effect, almost like watercolor. The angels holding candles on page 14, are done on the #14 (14 threads to the inch) Aida cloth.

WOOLS Wools can be used in all varieties, from Paternayan and Appleton to rug wool or knitting worsteds. Cotton floss also comes in all varieties—6-stranded, mercerized cotton ("DMC" in this type has a lovely sheen) or very shiny cotton twist. A lovely cotton thread with a very matte finish is Danish flower thread.

GOLD AND SILVER METAL THREADS Metal threads are varied, from braids and ribbons to fine lurex that can be stitched by hand or machine and then laundered. Most of today's metal threads are based on aluminum and are, therefore, nontarnishing. A wide variety of silver threads has been used in the candelabrum on page 80—they will gleam in the candlelight and never need polishing!

PATCHWORK FABRICS It's essential to store a collection of patchwork fabrics because they are like an artist's pallette—an array of colors in darks and lights ready to make a quilted fabric "painting," such as the Nativity Scene on page 92. Fabrics that are 100% cotton are easiest to work with because they "hold the fold" well when you crease down turnbacks. Don't forget, too, all those wonderfully useful "crafty" things like dacron batting, permanently soft and springy; foam core board for lightweight mounting; felt for padding and raising metal threads. For fine wire work, such as the support for the angel's halo (page 54), plastic bag ties, paper-covered fine wire, are indispensable.

What is more exciting than the ceiling-high pine standing in the corner of the room waiting for its lights and decorations?! You can make a high-fashion color scheme with everything in red and gold, or blue and silver—or all glittering white. But if you're like me, you'll find it irresistible to bring out all the old treasures from year to year, adding them to the new; and so your tree, though it may not be a decorator's delight, becomes the most beautiful, individual, and personal one in the world.

O TANNENBAUM!
O TANNENBAUM!

11

GNOMES

Bright red gnomes with white hats and pompons can hide, one by one, among the tree branches or hold hands to dance in rows around it, as you see on the previous page. Or they could hang as a Christmas mobile in a child's room (opposite). But who is to say at which year childhood ends? In our family we hang them around a bunch of mistletoe in the hall at Christmastime to greet us cheerfully whenever we come through the front door!

Materials

#10 plastic canvas (available by the yard; 6 gnomes can be cut from ½ yard)
Persian wool (separate the 3-strand yarn and use 2 strands)
Pompon cut from ¾" circle

Order of Working

With a permanent marker, outline rectangles 29 x 34 holes on the canvas. You can mark rows of rectangles leaving one hole open between each in order to establish the area for each gnome and to make counting them out from the graph easier. Following the graph, start

at the top center with the white cap, and work down row by row in tent stitch, using pale peach color for the face, red for the body, and peach for the hands. As the reverse side will be showing, keep everything very neat, carefully concealing your beginning and ending threads under the previous stitches.

Work the features in back stitch and the buttons in French knots on the top, afterward.

Now, with sharp scissors, cut close around the stitching so that no plastic canvas shows beyond the edges. For a simple effect, leave the edges unbound; but if you prefer, bind them in a simple lacing stitch in matching color. Make a pompon by winding wool around 2 cardboard discs. When it is completely covered, cut the wool all around, sliding the points of the scissors between the cardboard. Now wrap and tie the wool tightly between the discs. Trim into a neat ball and sew it invisibly in place on the gnome's head. To hang up each gnome, use the thread used for tying the pompon. Sew the hands together to join them in a straight line, which naturally rolls in on itself to form the ring shown, opposite.

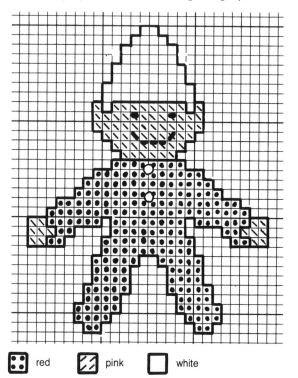

red   pink   white

CROSS-STITCH ANGELS

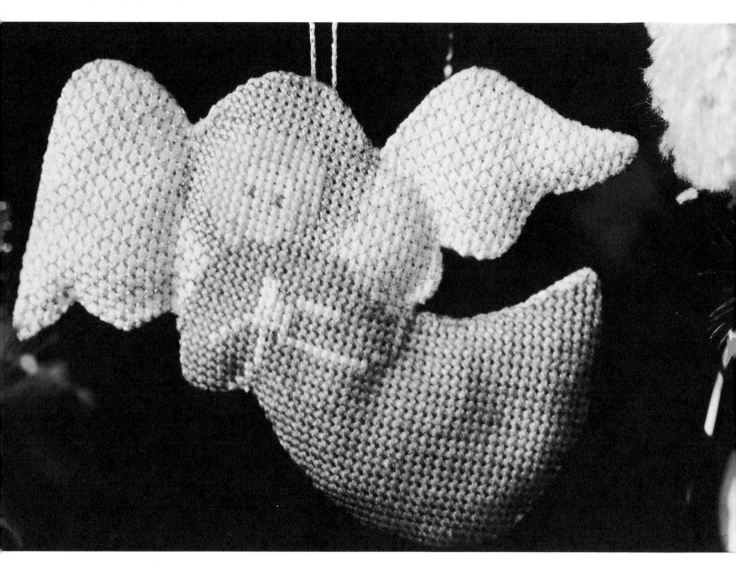

Gold-haloed angels with silver wings can be worked with bright or pastel robes, all in simple cross stitch. You could maintain this soft, padded look for the decoration of a whole tree, if you made little cross-stitch "pillows" just like the angels—in the shapes of sun, moon, stars, silver clouds, and rainbows.

MATERIALS

DMC cotton floss
Aida cloth, cream-colored, 14 threads to the inch
Dacron batting
Silver thread: DMC Fil d'argent

ORDER OF WORKING

Stretch Aida cloth in an embroidery frame—round or square—and count the cross stitches from the graph (opposite), working with 2 strands of cotton floss. Notice the diagram for cross stitch on the next page. The first row of stitches is taken with a vertical stitch on the back. The second row is stitched like needlepoint tent stitch, slanting the needle at the back. This uses more thread but looks more filled and close, with each stitch raised and clear-cut. Use 2 threads of silver and tie it with a single knot around the eye of the needle as you work, to prevent the slippery metal from constantly unthreading.

The back of the angel can be plain- or cross-stitched. (Follow the graph, reversing it and leaving out arms and face.) Sew the right sides together by hand or machine; turn inside out and stuff lightly with Dacron filling. Blind-stitch the opening closed. Suspend the finished angel from the back of her halo by silver thread.

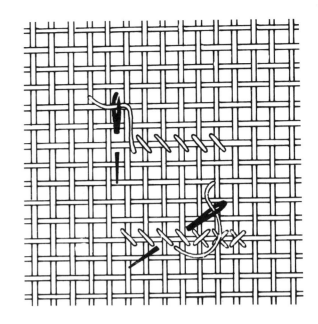

⊡ unworked		▣ orange	
⊡ flesh		△ blue	
⊞ white		⊙ yellow	
▨ rose		⧄ silver	
◪ pink		⊠ gold	

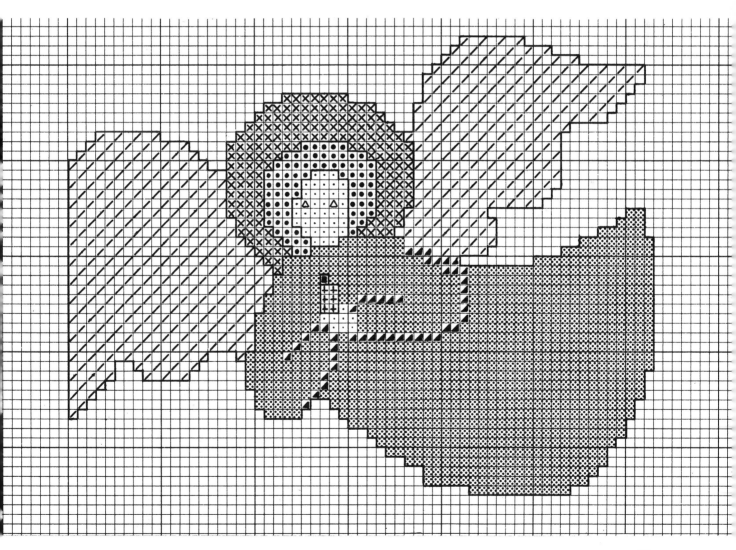

SILVER STARS AND SNOWFLAKES
(Color Plate 7)

With simple straight stitches in soft wool and silver thread, you can make flat or three-dimensional stars and snowflakes that will glisten on an all-white snowy tree.

MATERIALS

Plastic canvas (available by the sheet), size 10½" x 13½"

Plastic canvas (available by the yard), 10 holes to the inch

Super-white acrylic yarn (Nantuk is ideal weight and color)

Silver Lurex knitting or crochet thread (Camelot or similar)

ORDER OF WORKING

FLAT STAR *(bottom right of photo)*

Working on plastic canvas by the yard, 10 holes to the inch, and using one thread of white yarn, count the design from the diagram, starting in the center. Complete the pattern using 2 threads of silver yarn to surround the white center motif. Alternately you can reverse the colors, working silver in the center, white on the outside. Keep the reverse side neat so that you can leave the star unbacked, since the light shining through creates a shimmery effect. When the design is complete, cut the canvas one thread beyond the stitching (see snowflake diagram) and bind the edges with a whipping stitch (see diagram, page 158).

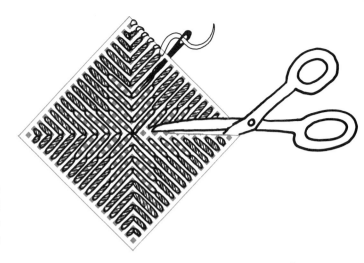

3-DIMENSIONAL STAR *(far left in photo)*

For greater rigidity for this star, use sheets of plastic canvas, 7 holes to the inch. To keep the stars approximately the same size as the flat one, on this larger canvas, work the center star over 4 threads instead of 7. Work two of these stars the same size, leaving a row of unworked holes on each so that a slit can be cut from the point of the square to the center without the threads unraveling (see diagram). Whip-

stitch the edges and slide the two stars together interlocking them at the slits, so that they hold together at 45° angles to one another.

SNOWFLAKE

(upper left and right, lower right in photo)

The snowflakes are worked in the same way as the flat star, using #10 canvas and following the diagram. When complete, cut the canvas all around slightly beyond the stitching and leave unbound.

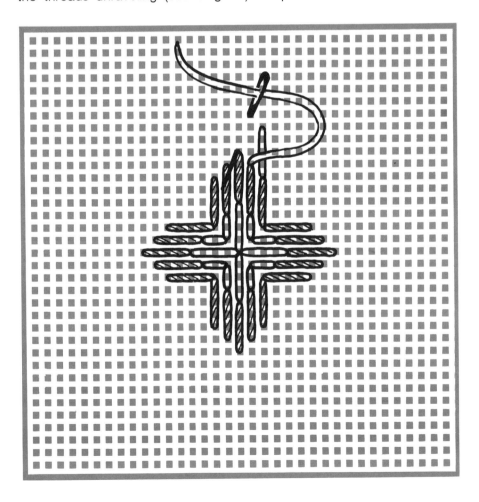

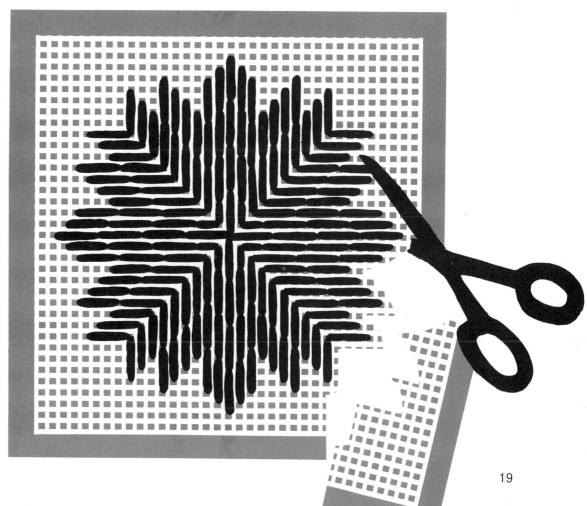

BEATRIX POTTER FELT ORNAMENTS

Beatrix Potter's delightful animals have always been favorites of anyone who has ever held a needle—and stitching them for the tree on white felt in cotton floss is delightfully simple. Large areas are left unworked for a light, open effect, and the red felt backing is cut larger so it projects beyond the edges and frames each one against the green tree.

MATERIALS

Felt, red and white
Cotton floss
Dacron batting

ORDER OF WORKING

Trace the life-size designs from these pages and, using carbon or Fusible web (page 154), transfer them to the white felt. Using 4 threads of cotton floss, follow the suggestions for color and stitch (for stitches see pages 25, 156–158). If you prefer, use your own ideas to create original techniques and combinations. When the stitching is complete, cut out each animal, leaving ¼″ extra felt all around as an edging beyond the outline. Cut a red felt backing ¼″ larger still.

Backstitch the finished animal and the red backing together along the outline. Pad lightly, sew up the opening, and hang from the tree by a loop of silver or gold thread.

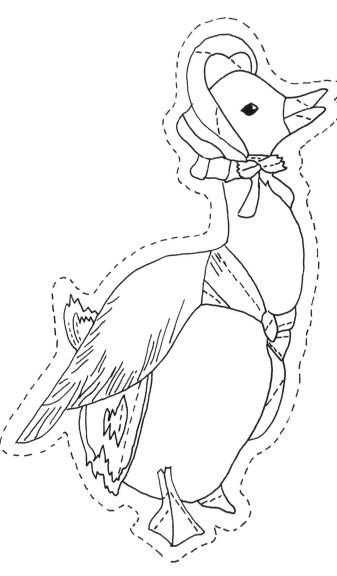

JEMIMA PUDDLEDUCK		
	Color	**Stitch**
Head and body	light, dark gray	stem outline
Bonnet	dark turquoise	satin stitch
Wing	light, dark gray	stem stitch
Shawl	pink, lilac	long and short
Beak and feet	yellow	satin stitch

KNITTING MOUSE

	Color	Stitch
Chair	dark brown	satin stitch and stem outline
Dress	shades of pink	squared filling
Shawl	shades of blue	long and short
Knitting	green	raised stem
Head	dark, light brown	long and short

PETER RABBIT

	Color	Stitch
Fur	dark, medium brown	long and short
Coat	light, dark blue	long and short
Tail	white	turkey work
Feet	gold metallic	satin stitch
Features	black, pink	satin stitch

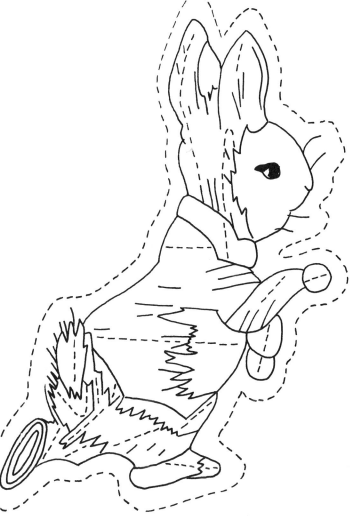

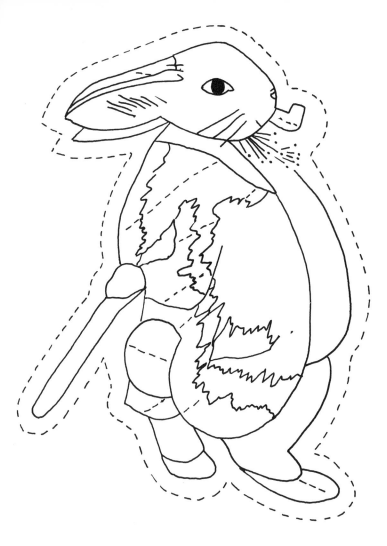

BENJAMIN BUNNY

	Color	Stitch
Coat	lilac, blue	long and short
Head	dark, light brown	stem stitch
Feet	pink	satin stitch
Tail	white	satin stitch
Walking stick	brown	back stitch
Bow tie	red	satin stitch

HUNCA MUNCA

	Color	Stitch
Chair	brown	satin stitch
Head	dark, light brown	stem stitch
Skirt	lilac, dark pink	stem outlines
Apron	orange, red	lazy daisy flowers
		French knot centers
	aqua	squared filling
Baby	pinks, browns	backstitch
		French knots
Tails	brown	slanting satin
Eyes	black	padded satin

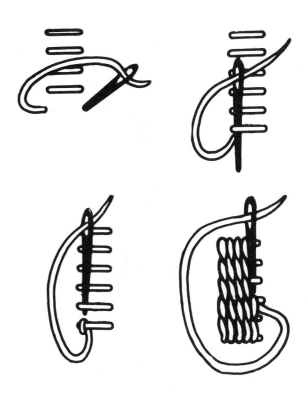

Raised stem stitch

Long and short stitch

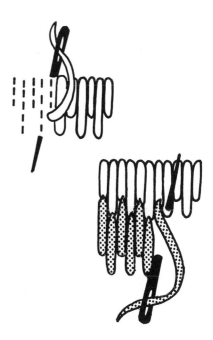

AMIABLE GUINEA PIG

	Color	Stitch
Coat	orange	satin stitch
Tie	blue	satin stitch
Head	light, medium brown	long and short
Hat	dark, light brown	Long and short
	black	stem outline
Waistcoat	lilac	outline in back-stitch
	black	French knots
Legs	yellow	long and short
Ears	pink	satin stitch

BEATRIX POTTER
NEEDLEPOINT ORNAMENTS

Your favorite Beatrix Potter characters can become like little jeweled medallions in needlepoint. You can achieve a detailed effect by combining crewel and needlepoint stitches on a #14 canvas, using long vertical straight stitches, brick stitch, and, in some places, outlining with 1 or 2 threads of black cotton floss.

MATERIALS

#14 interlocked canvas (12 ornaments can be
   cut from ¼ yard)
Persian wool
Cotton floss
Felt for backing
Dacron batting

ORDER OF WORKING

Using a permanent marker, trace the outline shown on this page to the canvas. Make sure the dotted line running through the center of your design is lined up with the vertical threads of your canvas. All the ornaments are worked in simple vertical satin stitch, using 1 thread of wool in the colors indicated on pages 22 and 24. Come up at one side and go down at the other on the lines you have traced. Work areas with brick stitch (stitches on pages 35, 156–157). Complete the background in continental stitch, working right up to the satin stitches, to make a close, neat transition where the two stitches join. Now outline in backstitch with 3 threads of black cotton, as indicated by bold black lines on the diagram. Finally, work features—whiskers and tails—in some cases working right on top of the previous stitches. Cut out the finished oval, leaving ¼″ turnbacks all around. Snip and baste turnbacks to reverse side. Cut out red felt ¼″ larger all around, then hem needlepoint in place on the felt backing, leaving 1″ open for stuffing. Lightly stuff with batting, close opening, and edge with a close braid, which forms the hanger at the same time (as in the photo).

NOËL BOXES

Instead of Jack, put *snowmen* in boxes—white, fluffy snowmen with red or black felt hats. They can sit in green boxes with red-and-white peppermint-striped letters cut out of plastic canvas. A row of them spelling "Happy Holidays" could be arranged on the mantelpiece, or hang them in the window or march them up the staircase. A single one with a friend's initial could be a special way to give that small-and-special gift. And of course the snowmen will always be delighted to hang on the tree—perhaps as holders for miniature candy canes.

MATERIALS

#10 plastic canvas for letters
#7 plastic canvas sheets (2 boxes from 1 sheet)
Persian wool or Nantuk acrylic yarn
Felt
Pompon makers (optional)

ORDER OF WORKING

SNOWMEN

Make 2 pompons in white Nantuk, using plastic pompon makers or cardboard circles and following the directions shown on page 158—one, 2" in diameter for the body, and one, 1½" for the head. Sew two pompons together and glue on eyes, nose, and hats to the smaller pompon of the two. Braid 3 or 4 strands of yarn for a scarf.

BOXES

Cut #7 plastic canvas 12 threads by 12 threads—6 pieces for each box. Stitch in brick stitch

28

(page 157) or tent stitch (page 35) in bright green. Stitch letters according to graph on #10 plastic canvas in bright red and white. Cut out in shape, and with sewing thread sew them onto the center of one square of the box. Join the pieces of the box with binding stitch (see page 158), leaving the top open on 3 sides. Finish the raw edges of the lid and box with binding stitch. Line top of box with green felt.

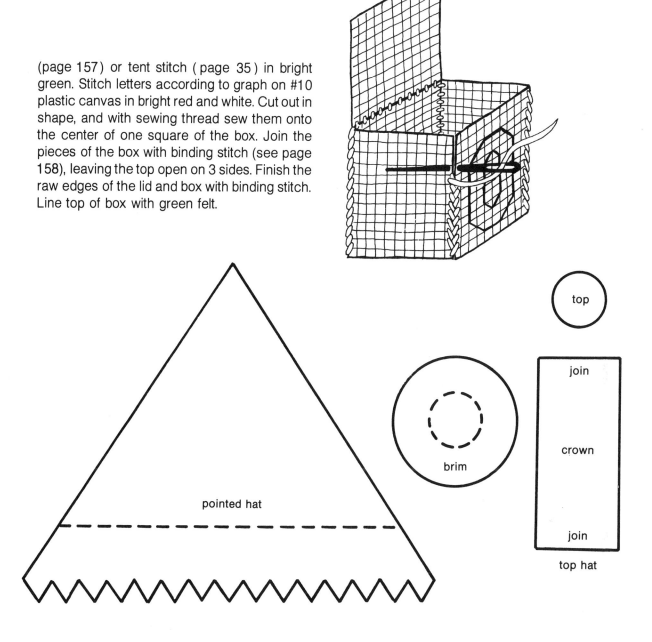

pointed hat

top

brim

join

crown

join

top hat

• red   □ white

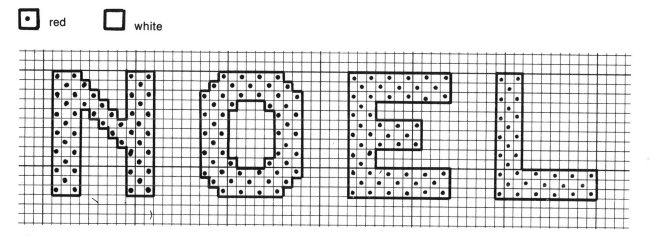

DIAMOND CUBES

These cubes made of plastic canvas diamonds will always look trim and perfect because the canvas never loses its shape. They can be used just as they are, to add bright spots of color and glitter to your tree, or 3 of the upper edges of each one can be left open to form little boxes with lids perfect for concealing small surprises such as toys or candies.

MATERIALS

Precut diamond-shaped plastic canvas or
   plastic sheets
4-ply Nantuk acrylic yarn
Gold and silver Camelot metallic yarn

ORDER OF WORKING

For the cubes shown here, cut diamond-shapes or #7 plastic canvas so that each diamond is 11 threads by 11 threads. You can vary the size according to your preference—just make sure that the thread count on all sides is equal. Six diamonds make up one cube.

With 1 strand of Nantuk or 2 strands of Camelot, fill in the diamonds with a simple vertical stitch over 1 thread of the canvas. The pattern and color combinations are endless. Work in stripes, concentric diamonds, or the simple flower pattern shown on the left.

When the six sides are completed, join them as shown with the whipping stitch.

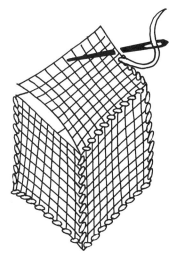

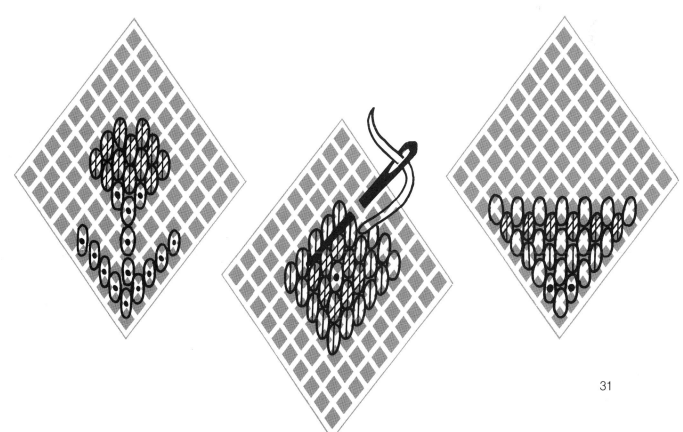

TWINKLE, TWINKLE, LITTLE STAR

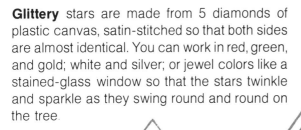

Glittery stars are made from 5 diamonds of plastic canvas, satin-stitched so that both sides are almost identical. You can work in red, green, and gold; white and silver; or jewel colors like a stained-glass window so that the stars twinkle and sparkle as they swing round and round on the tree.

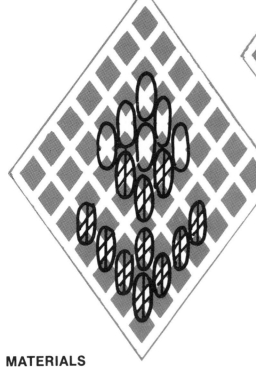

MATERIALS

Precut diamond-shaped plastic canvas or
Nantuk acrylic yarn, Persian wool, or knitting
  worsted
Camelot metallic thread, gold or silver

ORDER OF WORKING

Begin by cutting the diamond-shapes so that each of the five small diamonds has 7 holes along each side. Choose one of the two patterns shown here and work 5 identical diamonds, following the graph. (Begin and end the threads by running them invisibly into the previous stitches.) Lace the diamonds together, as shown, edge the star with the same whipping stitch, and use wool or metal thread as a loop hanger. By varying the colors in each of the patterns you can create an almost unlimited variety of lively designs.

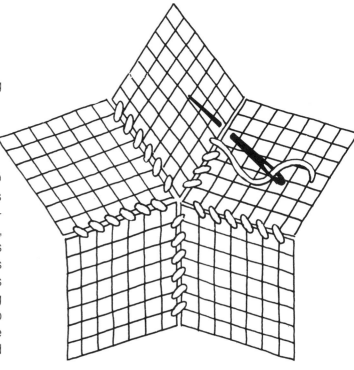

NEEDLEPOINT STOCKING ORNAMENTS

The perfect gift for a friend is a miniature needle-point stocking to hang on the tree, showing his or her favorite hobby or occupation—whether it's skiing, disco, jogging, or merely drinking champagne! You can use the designs on these pages to get started, but once you have the idea, you can find suitable animals in children's books and combine them with anything that will make them completely personal. By following the graphs you can work them in needlepoint or, alternatively, in cross stitch.

MATERIALS

Mono canvas #18—¼ yard (40″ wide) for 8 stockings (needlepoint)
Red felt for backing—½ yard for 6 stockings (needlepoint)
3-strand Persian wool (use 1 strand for needle-point)
Aida cloth #14 (cross stitch)
6-strand cotton floss (use 2 strands for cross stitch)
Prefolded seam binding

ORDER OF WORKING

Trace the pattern outline and work in tent stitch, placing colors as desired. Block needlepoint. Cut out stocking leaving a ½″ turnback all around. Fold under turnback at top of stocking and stitch in place. Cut out matching piece of red felt for backing. With right sides out, baste stocking to felt, leaving top edges free. Trim seam to ¼″. Stitch prefolded seam binding around basted edges and across top of stocking, leaving a loop long enough for hanging. For instructions on working cross stitch on Aida cloth, see pages 14–15.

Tent stitch (continental)

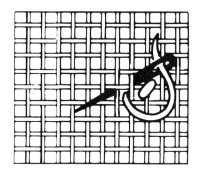

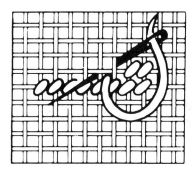

Tent stitch (basketweave)

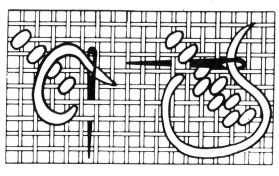

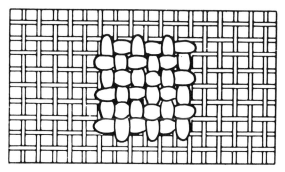

reverse side

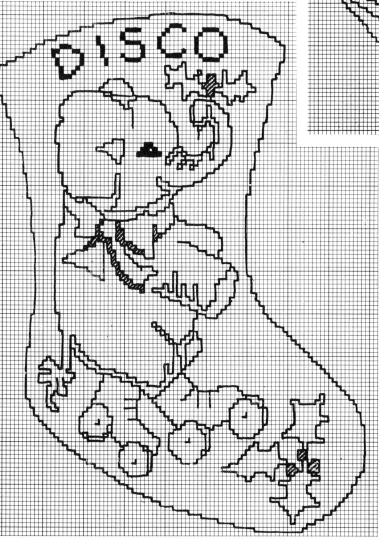

37

CREWEL BUTTERFLIES

Silken butterflies look as if they are enameled in bright shiny colors—red and green, blue and turquoise, orange and lemon—all enriched with the gleam of couched gold threads. Work back and front in different colors, if you like the effect or real butterflies with contrasting underwings.

MATERIALS

Fine-weave linen or cotton fabric
Cotton embroidery floss in assorted bright
    colors
Japanese gold
Maltese silk waxed with beeswax

ORDER OF WORKING

Transfer the life-size designs onto the linen, using the light box or carbon-paper method (page 154). Trace two for each butterfly—one front and one back.

Using 4 strands of cotton, fill in each area with satin stitch (see page 156 for stitch instructions). Work the blocks of color to touch one another, so that the stitches share the same holes. When all satin stitching is complete, couch down 2 strands of Japanese gold where the colors join, sewing the metal thread down with a single strand of waxed silk. Cut out the front and back, leaving ¼" turnbacks all around. Fold back turnbacks and, with wrong sides facing, sew together with an overcast stitch, leaving one section open for padding. Stuff with batting, sew up opening, and cover the seam by couching 2 strands of Japanese gold around the edge of the butterfly. Make a twisted cord, as shown, using 4 six-strand threads of cotton floss. To make a cord, knot 2 single lengths of wool together at each end. Secure one end to any firm object. Insert a pencil at the other end (see diagram) and turn it to twist the wool until you have a single tightly twisted length of wool. Then fold it in half, allow the wool to twist back on itself into a nice thick cord, stroke it smooth, and knot the open end. Sew a tassel to one end of the cord (see page 158) and, with a large needle, draw through the center of the butterfly, leaving the tassel below and sufficient cord above for hanging the butterfly, as in the photo.

MR. AND MRS. MOUSE

Little gray mice in bright red coats can continue the idea of individualized Christmas ornaments —you can dress one to represent each member of the family! Once you have the basic bodies stitched, the clothing can be varied to make the mice into skiers, golfers, sailors, etc., for there's no end to the fun you can have with them.

MATERIALS

Felt and cardboard
Dacron batting
Embroidery floss
"Found" objects such as beads, feathers, fur, lace, etc., as you need them

ORDER OF WORKING

Cut out all of the shapes according to the patterns on the following page. Because they are worked in felt, turnbacks are not necessary.

Work the eyes in satin stitch, using 6 strands of black embroidery floss. To assemble, place the pink inner ear at the base of the gray outer ear and with an overcast stitch sew them in place. Again with the overcast stitch sew the two sides of the mouse together, stuffing them with Dacron batting as you sew. Once the body of the mouse is complete, join it to one piece of the base (placement is noted by a dotted line). Cut lightweight cardboard slightly smaller than the base and sandwich it between the two base pieces. Join these together with an overcast stitch.

The mouse is now ready to be dressed. Fold over the sleeve and sew across the bottom seam. Pull the arm through the sleeve. Sew each garment separately and dress the mouse as you would a doll. Pull the sleeves through the cut openings in the coat and tack them in place. Sew on tail. Satin-stitch the nose over the seam with 6 strands of black floss. To work the whiskers, thread 3 strands of black floss and pull through on either side of the nose as indicated; center, and trim to about 2".

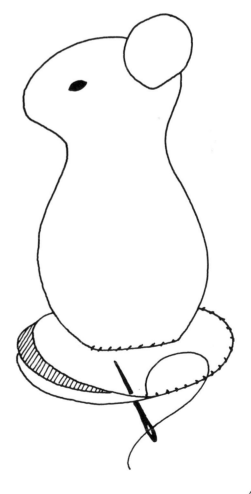

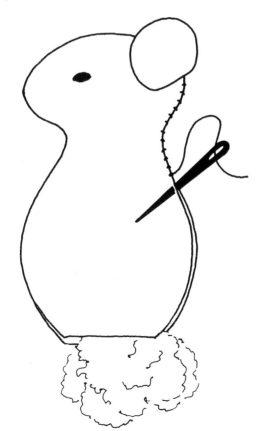

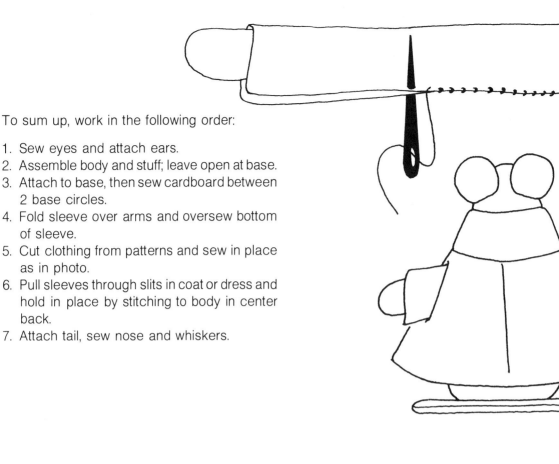

To sum up, work in the following order:

1. Sew eyes and attach ears.
2. Assemble body and stuff; leave open at base.
3. Attach to base, then sew cardboard between 2 base circles.
4. Fold sleeve over arms and oversew bottom of sleeve.
5. Cut clothing from patterns and sew in place as in photo.
6. Pull sleeves through slits in coat or dress and hold in place by stitching to body in center back.
7. Attach tail, sew nose and whiskers.

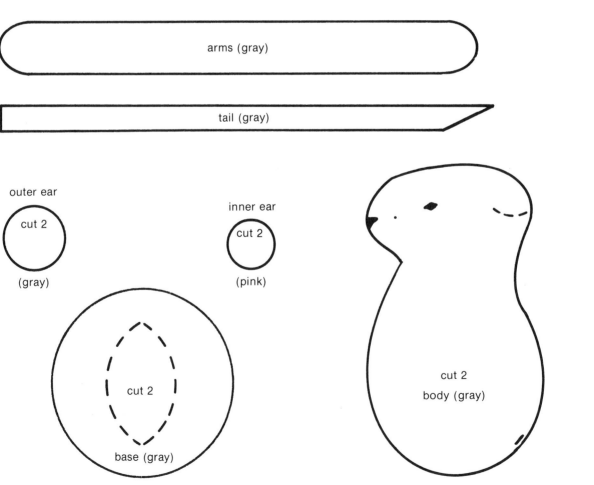

arms (gray)

tail (gray)

outer ear

cut 2

(gray)

inner ear

cut 2

(pink)

cut 2

base (gray)

cut 2
body (gray)

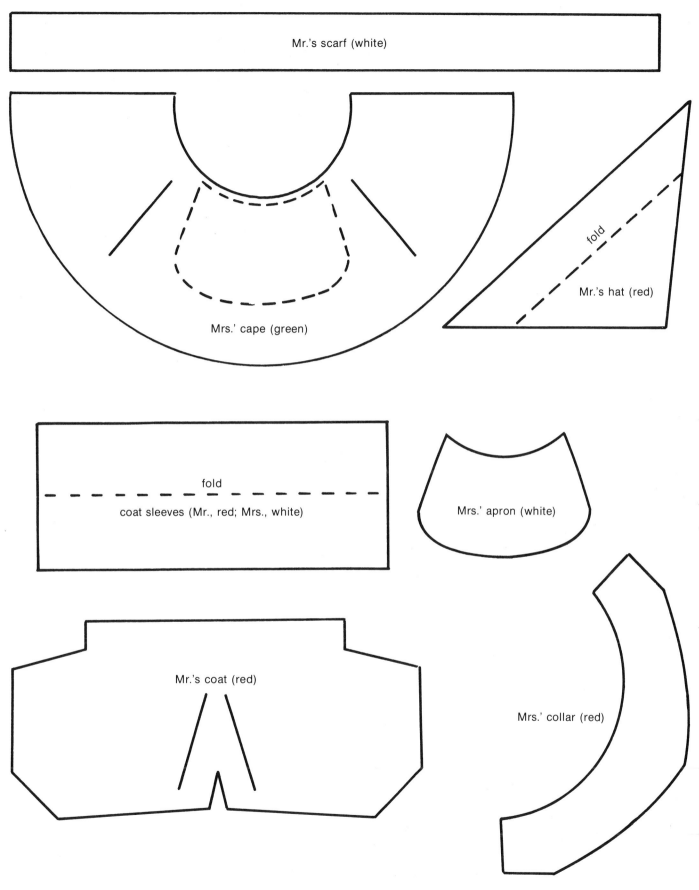

Mr.'s scarf (white)

Mrs.' cape (green)

fold

Mr.'s hat (red)

fold

coat sleeves (Mr., red; Mrs., white)

Mrs.' apron (white)

Mr.'s coat (red)

Mrs.' collar (red)

43

CHESSIE® AND PLAYMATES

Chessie and her playmates are so well known that they hardly need any introduction. The sleeping kitten was adopted by the Chesapeake and Ohio Railway as their mascot and trademark in the 1920s. Since then Chessie has enchanted people everywhere, sleeping contentedly between her white sheets. Here she is shown as a tree ornament, stitched in cotton floss on white felt, and on page 104 you will find her as a door pillow.

MATERIALS

Cotton floss
Felt
Dacron batting

ORDER OF WORKING

Trace and transfer the life-size designs on these pages by the method described on page 154. Following the stitch diagrams on page 25, work all the fur in long and short stitch, using 4 strands of floss. After stitching the ears and paws, work all around the outer edge of the face. Start on top of the head, and work down towards the nose. Work the dark gray first, next the medium gray shades, then fill in with light gray. Work the white stitching around the eyes and mouth, and then satin-stitch the features with turquoise eyes outlined in black backstitch. The finishing touches are the whiskers in black straight stitch and the sheets in gray backstitch. Finish the ornaments like the ones on page 27, edging them with a bright red chain-stitch border (page 46) instead of a braid.

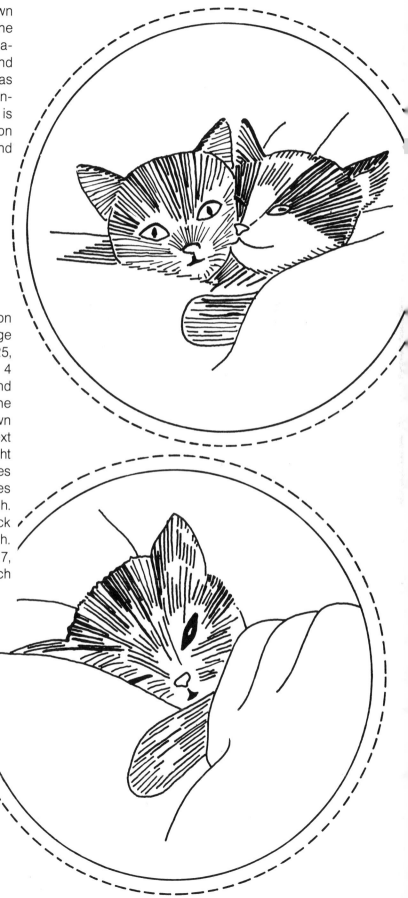

GOLDEN BIRDS

Red, blue, or white felt showing through between the gold sequins on each bird's wing makes these Christmas ornaments festive and colorful.

MATERIALS

Red, white, or blue felt
Gold sequins and 2 blue sequins for eyes
Gold Camelot yarn
Cotton floss, yellow and black

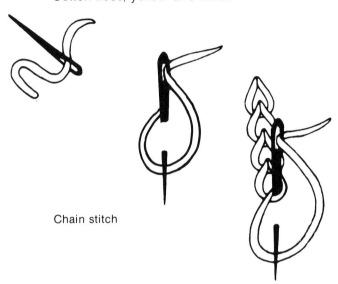

Chain stitch

ORDER OF WORKING

(1) With gold Camelot yarn, work slightly spaced rows of chain stitch to cover the body, as shown in the diagram. (2) Using 3 strands of yellow floss, work the beak in satin stitch at the same angle as the dotted lines in the diagram. (3) With 3 strands of matching cotton floss, work a single row of stem stitch, outlining the wing. Work another row of stem stitch in gold Camelot yarn just inside the first row and around the top of the wing. (4) Attach the sequins to the wing and eyes with a French knot (using 4 strands of cotton floss). (5) Cut out both sides of the bird along the cutting line. With the wrong sides facing, fold in a small seam allowance and oversew the two pieces together. Leave a small opening and loosely stuff with batting or scrap yarn. Continue oversewing. (6) With 1 strand of matching floss, sew down a strand of gold Camelot to cover the seam.

46

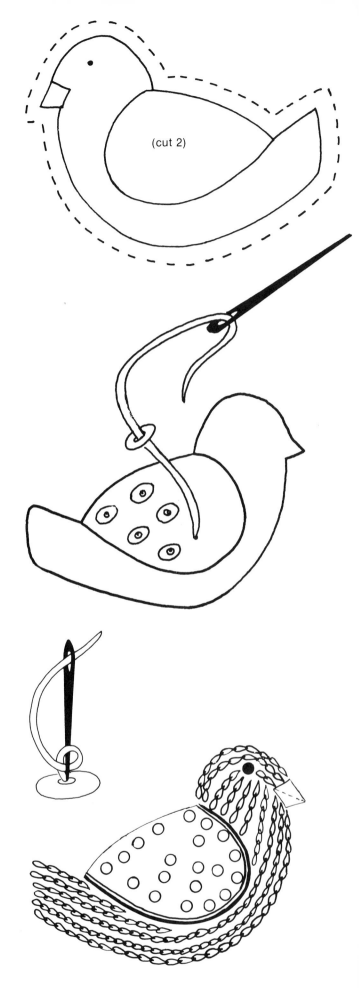

(cut 2)

EYE OF GOD

Ojos de Dios, or Eyes of God, have probably been in use since the time of Cleopatra. This way of winding threads around two crossed sticks is simple and effective. Use toothpicks, dowels, wooden skewers, or even long match sticks to get your effect, combining different threads and experimenting with different sizes.

MATERIALS

Toothpicks, wooden skewers, etc. (If you are using dowels, sharpen both ends in the pencil sharpener to give them a smooth finish, and with a razor blade, notch the center of each so they will fit snugly together when held at right angles.)

Colored cotton floss
Knitting worsted

ORDER OF WORKING

Hold the end of an uncut skein of cotton floss with your thumb and forefinger along one side of the toothpick (the end will be wrapped and secured as you work).

Wrap under and over the first toothpick, going right around it once (pulling it snug).

Go on to the next toothpick and repeat, wrapping right around it once again.

As you work around and around, always wrapping *under,* then over, you will see that the wrapped toothpicks stand out from the background of thread, which by now holds the cross firmly in place.

Wrap all 4 sticks 12 times, then change colors by holding the last end of thread alongside one toothpick and the new thread beside it.

Wrap with the new thread, pulling it snug to secure the ends of both the old and new thread without tying a knot. With the new color, wrap *over,* then under, the toothpick—exactly the reverse of your first weaving. This will give you the effect of flat weaving on the front, and the wrapped toothpicks will appear on the reverse side of the ornament.

Continue, reversing the wrapping and changing the colors until the toothpicks are almost covered. Leave at least ¼" projecting so the threads don't slip off the ends. Knot the thread in a loop around the last toothpick so that the thread forms a tie to hang it on the tree.

Now that you've mastered the basics, you'll find there are all kinds of wonderful variations. Work in bold scale with silver and gold cords and super-white knitting worsted, gluing a golden ball to each of the 4 ends. There are variations in the wrapping, too. You can try wrapping the whole cross in the same way without changing color or direction. You can try wrapping over 4 crossed rods instead of 2, and you can lay long threads of colored wool along the rods before you begin, so that they are held by the wrapping in the middle but project to form tassels at the four ends.

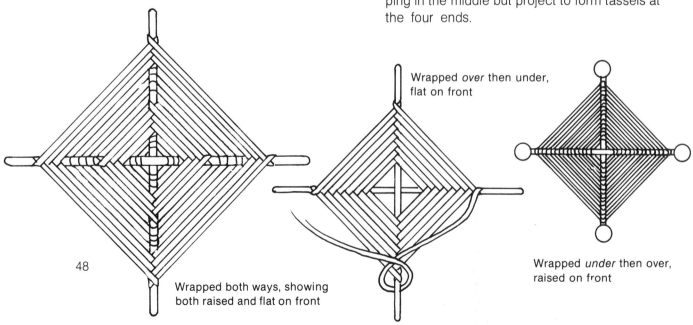

Wrapped *over* then under, flat on front

Wrapped both ways, showing both raised and flat on front

Wrapped *under* then over, raised on front

LACE SNOWBALLS

These airy lace snowballs are so quick to make you can almost start the day before Christmas and have them on the tree in time. They are done with lace, molded on any round shape, such as a grapefruit, then painted with white glue and joined with narrow lace trim round their "equator." You can hang them up with ribbons, with a silver bell or tiny white Christmas light in the center. You can use antique lace and velvet ribbons or inexpensive lace trim from the dime store—they look sensational either way.

MATERIALS

Lace banding approximately 4″ wide
Narrow lace trim
Sobo or Elmer's glue or Argo cornstarch
Ribbons
Small grapefruit, orange, child's plastic ball, or
  balloon shape to use as a mold
Masking tape

ORDER OF WORKING

Wrap 4″ wide lace around the center of the mold and hold it in place around the circumference with masking tape. Dart or gather the extra fabric in at the top, and paint all over with glue or starch to which a little water has been added. (A dressmaker's tailor's chalk pencil with a stiff brush at the end is a good tool for applying it.) Repeat for the other half, using the same mold or another one of the same size. Allow to dry overnight. When dry, pry the firm lace loose with a grapefruit knife, and lift off the mold. Lightly stitch the two halves together (page 158), and cover the join with narrow lace, a frilled lace trim, or a lace insertion with ribbon run through it. Attach bows of ribbon at the top and bottom of the snowball. Push a tiny white light through the hole left by the gathering thread at the top—or hang a silver bell inside, if the lace is transparent. You can also make a lace ball by wrapping narrow lace around and

around the mold, crossing over at the top and bottom, and stretching it evenly. After gluing it firmly in position and allowing it to dry, carefully cut around the circumference, pry the lace loose and remove the mold, and finish in the same way as suggested above.

CLOTHESPIN ANGELS

With the most inexpensive materials, you can make a flock of charming little angels dressed in white eyelet with lacy wings and golden halos. You can arrange them on a swag of pine branches along the mantelpiece or you can let them hold hands around the tree—just like the gnomes on pages 12–13. The little ladies below came from England and are dressed in bright calicos with lace trim.

MATERIALS

Clothespins
Pipe cleaners
White eyelet edging
Bands of lace
Wool thread
Gold metal thread
Felt
Ribbon

ORDER OF WORKING

Begin by firmly twisting a pipe cleaner just under the knob of a clothespin, so that two "arms" project equally on either side. Paint a face on the knob with magic markers, or enamel or oil paint; twist some wool and glue it in place for hair. Then gather some white eyelet for a long-sleeved dress, cover the gathering at the neck with a narrow gathered strip of lace. Finally, attach wings made of folded lace and, if you wish, a golden halo made like the one for the treetop angel on page 54.

TREETOP ANGEL

(Color Plate 1)

In contrast to the clothespin angels, the treetop angel is more elaborate; in fact, it may become an heirloom to be brought out year after year. This singing angel has a dress made in an antique needlepoint pattern, white lacy pulled-work wings, and a golden prayerbook and halo couched with gold metal thread.

MATERIALS

Broad gold braid (for hair)
Gold thread (metallic cord)
#18 canvas (18 threads to the inch) for body
    and sleeves
#14 canvas for wings
Felt
Cotton floss
Beeswax
Wool thread and sewing silk
Plastic bag ties (paper-covered wire)

ORDER OF WORKING

HEAD. On pink felt, outline two head shapes from the pattern on this page. With 2 threads of cotton floss work eyes and cheeks in satin stitch, nose in straight stitch, and mouth in lazy daisy. Whip-stitch back and front together with opening at chin. Insert plastic bag tie and catch to back of head, leaving 3″ to 5″ extending. Now pad slightly. Cut out the felt neck from the pattern on this page and stitch into a tube. Thread the head wire through it and catch the neck into position on either side of the chin with a tiny invisible stitch (for stitches, see pages 156, 158).

HAIR. Wrap a bundle of gold braid around 3″ x 6″ cardboard. Slide it off the cardboard and backstitch the center of the loops to the middle of the head. Arrange the loops around the face and stitch them in 2 bundles at the back of the neck.

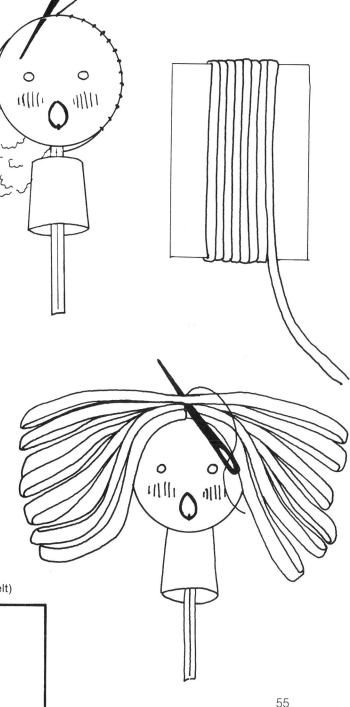

angel face (flesh felt)

angel neck (flesh felt)

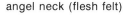

top

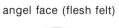

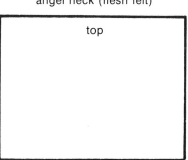

DRESS. Using a hard (H) pencil, mark a 12″ square on #18 needlepoint canvas. On paper, trace and cut out half the skirt pattern as shown on page 57. Line it up on the true diagonal of the canvas, as illustrated. Using a permanent marker, outline the pattern, then flip it over and trace the other side. Follow Color Plate 1, or make up your own color scheme, using 3 to 5 contrasting colors in each band. Starting at the bottom of the skirt with the first black line, follow the ribbon-pattern graph steps 1 through 5 to establish the first band of the pattern. Then work up, ribbon by ribbon, following diagram 6. (If you work on #18 canvas, you must repeat the 5-ribbon sequence, as it takes 14 ribbons to cover the dress.) Now seam the dress together down the center back, right sides facing. Fold back and hem the neck and base. Turn right sides out.

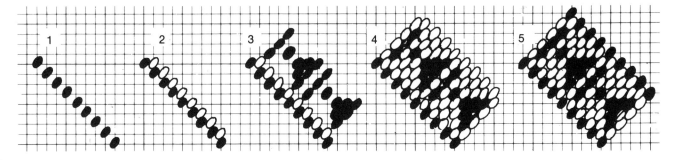

Ribbon pattern for skirt and sleeves

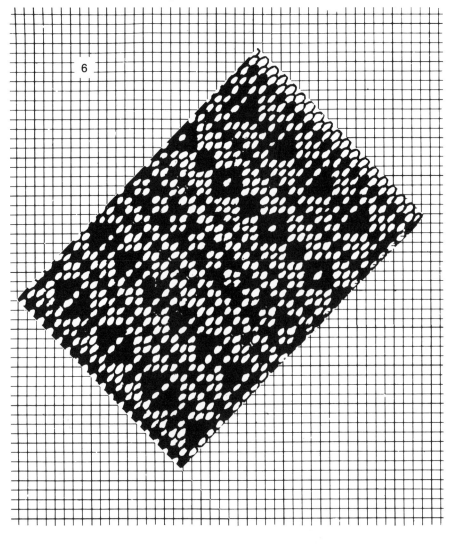

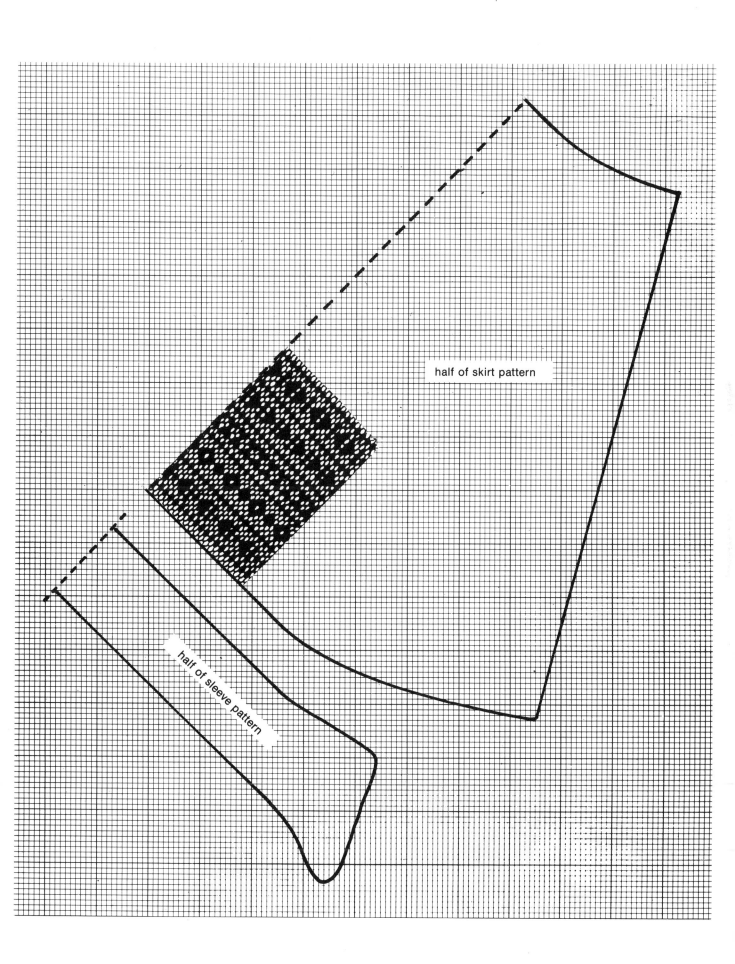

half of skirt pattern

half of sleeve pattern

SLEEVE. Trace half the sleeve pattern from page 57, flip it over, and trace the other side in the same way as the skirt. Work it in any of the ribbon patterns that you prefer, shown on the graph. (Refer again to Color Plate 1.) Whip-stitch the lower edges together as in the diagram, holding a strip of wire (or plastic bag tie) down the inside center as you go, in order to give the sleeve body. Attach the center back of the sleeves to the center seam of the dress slightly below the neck.

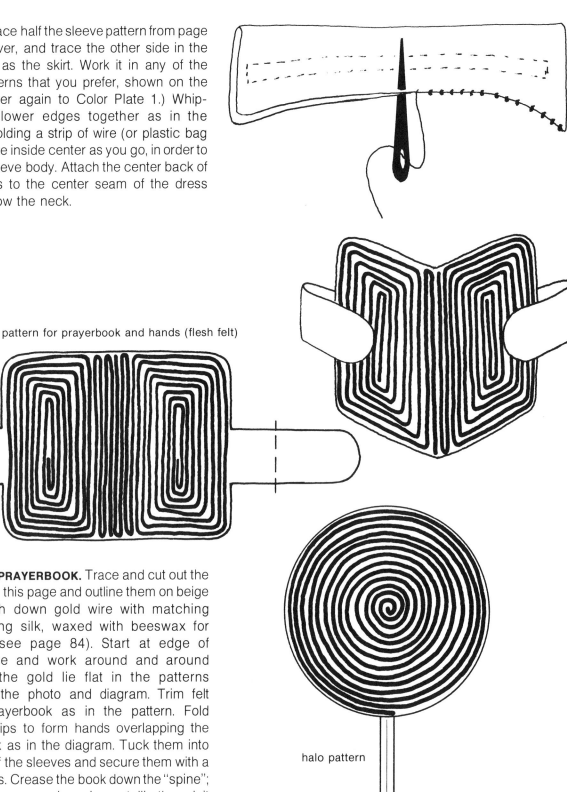

pattern for prayerbook and hands (flesh felt)

halo pattern

HALO AND PRAYERBOOK. Trace and cut out the patterns on this page and outline them on beige felt. Couch down gold wire with matching gold sewing silk, waxed with beeswax for strength (see page 84). Start at edge of each piece and work around and around to make the gold lie flat in the patterns shown in the photo and diagram. Trim felt around prayerbook as in the pattern. Fold back 2 strips to form hands overlapping the prayerbook as in the diagram. Tuck them into the ends of the sleeves and secure them with a few stitches. Crease the book down the "spine"; because you are using wire metallic thread, it will hold this position. Attach a plastic bag tie to the back of the halo.

WINGS. Outline the wings from the actual size pattern shown here, and work in pulled stitches as in diagram (Algerian eyelet, buttonhole, diamond lattice with satin stitch, see pages 156–157). When the pulled work is complete, couch a line of gold cord around the edge and trim the canvas close behind this cord, being careful not to cut your couching stitches.

ASSEMBLY

Stitch the head and halo plastic bag tie to the inside back of the dress. Lightly stitch a narrow gathered band of lace around the top of the dress to soften the neck. Finally, attach the center of the wings to the back of the dress and hold in place with a few small invisible stitches.

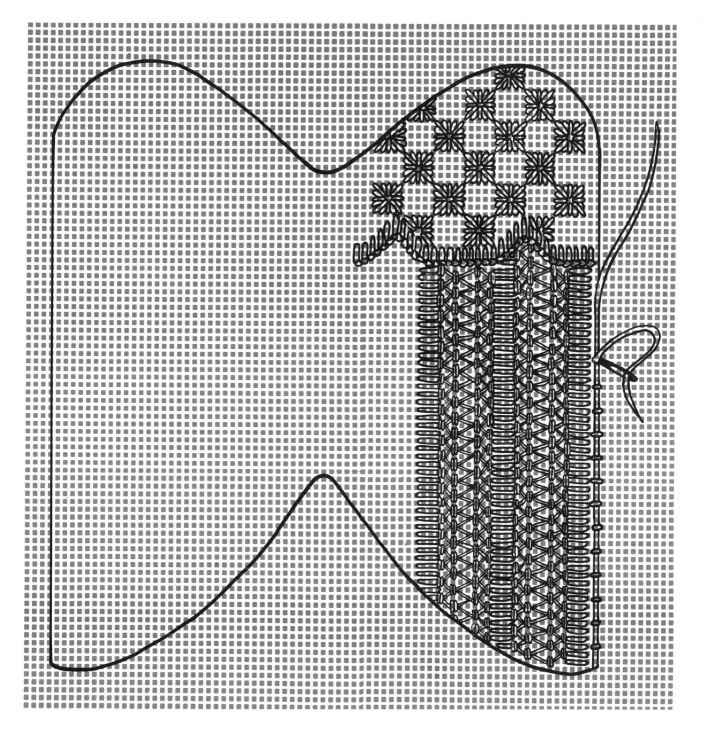

There are so many ways to make the house festive for the holidays, and on the following pages you'll find all kinds of ideas: guest towels, table linen, door pillows, for example, and most interesting of all, ways of combining your stitches with lighting. The silver candelabrum on page 80 can be your real masterpiece; the Kissenbaum can welcome you with its red candles; and the snowy village shown here, with little fairy lights glowing through the bright-colored windows, can make a splendid lighted centerpiece for the dining table or could look wonderful arranged around the base of the tree.

DECK THE HALLS

VILLAGE AND TREES
(Color Plate 4)

With plastic canvas you can build houses, churches, even an entire village to arrange under the tree. To design your own, cut the shapes out of graph paper and assemble them with masking tape—the only way to be sure your house is correct is to see it first three-dimensionally (see photo below).

MATERIALS

#10 plastic canvas for trees
#7 plastic canvas for houses
Nantuk acrylic yarn (see Color Plate 4 for colors, plus super-white for snow)

ORDER OF WORKING

To make the village shown, follow the cutting diagrams on the following pages. Complete each section before joining and work houses in brick stitch (page 157), bands of satin stitch (page 156), or tent stitch (page 35). Be sure to leave areas of the windows unworked for light to shine through. Trees on the house are worked in buttonhole stitch with French knots on top for snow. Work thick clumps of snow on the roofs in slanting satin stitch. Join and edge the pieces in binding stitch (page 158).

Trees are worked on #10 plastic canvas, which is flexible for curving. Cut out the three tree cone sections and work in bands of dark and lighter green buttonhole stitch (page 157). Sprinkle snow on cones with French knots, and at the tip of the upper cone work French knots on long stitches. Join each section to form cone and nest one on top of the other.

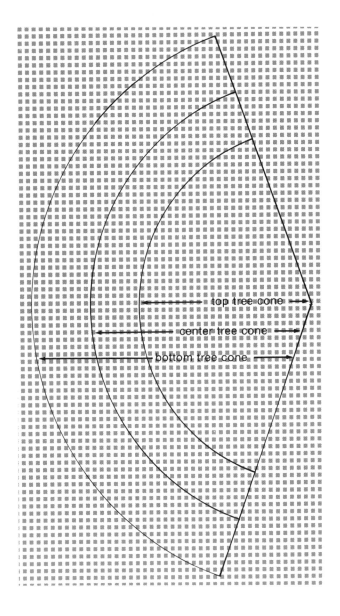

top tree cone
center tree cone
bottom tree cone

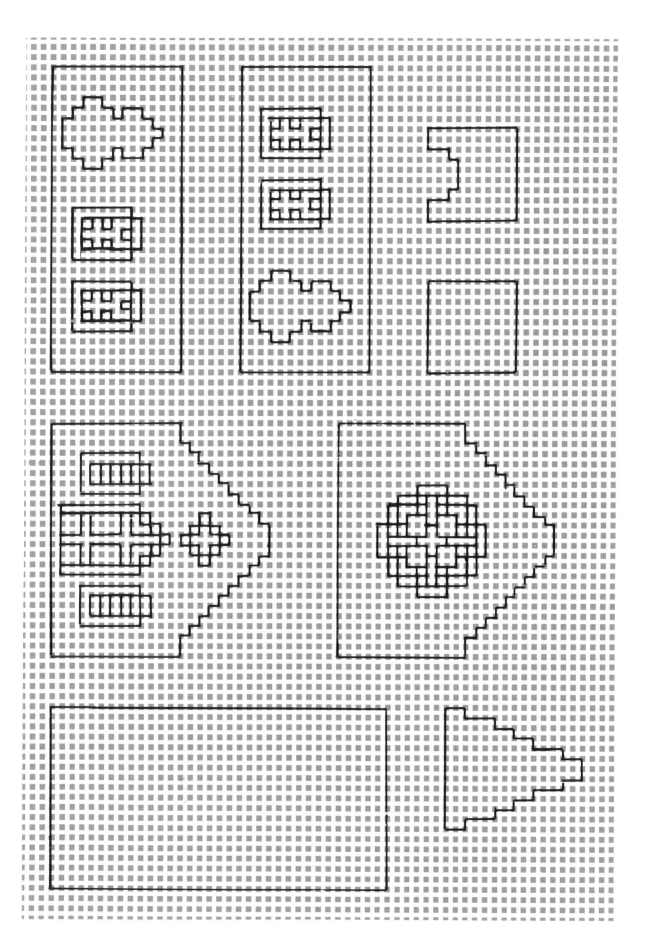

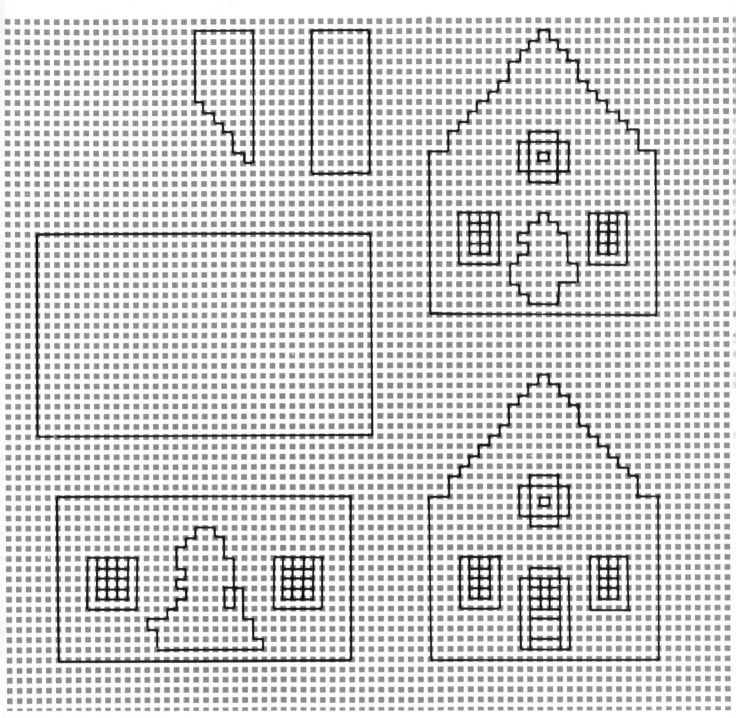

Diagrams for this project continue after color section.

64

Plate 1.   TREETOP ANGEL (page 55).

Plate 3.   KISSENBAUM with apples, ribbons, and electric lights (page 68).

Plate 2.   "O TANNENBAUM!" Erica's family Christmas tree.

Plate 5.   BEATRIX POTTER ANIMALS (page 114) with Erica's son, Illya, and a neighboring cat.

Plate 4.   SANTA IN A BALLOON over VILLAGE AND TREES (pages 138 and 62)

Plate 6.   Detail of SILVER CANDELABRUM (page 80).

Plate 7.   SILVER STARS AND SNOWFLAKES (page 17).

Plate 8.   QUILTED NATIVITY SCENE (page 92).

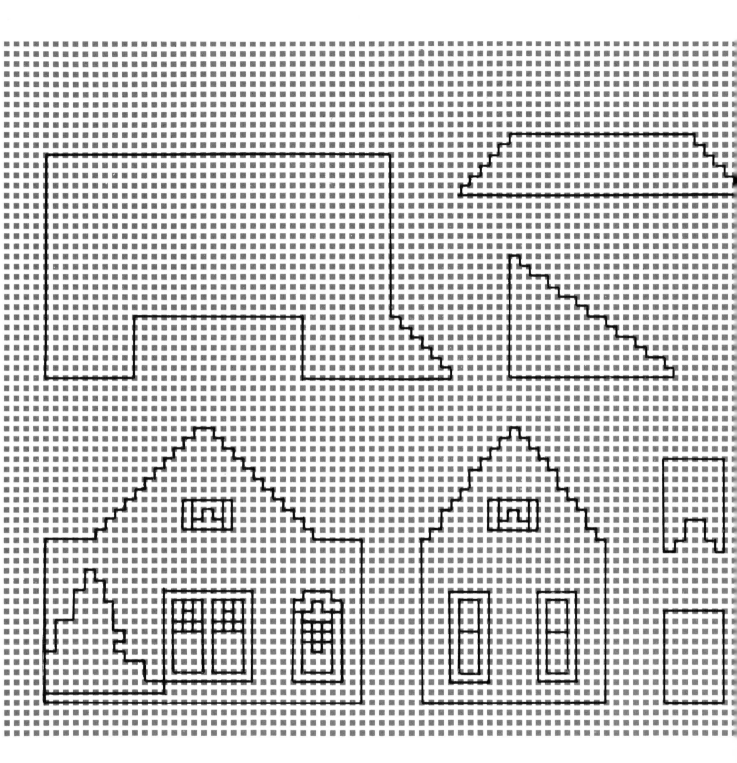

65

GIFT WREATH

Braided "tubes" of padded calico form the colorful foundation for a gift wreath—an original way of making a personal gift that's also a decoration. If your friend is a great chef, attach wooden spoons, an egg whisk, and a small silvery cheese grater to the braided wreath. If knitting is her "thing," tie on a skein of yarn and a bunch of knitting needles with a bright ribbon. And, of course, this is a natural for your stitching friends—you can decorate the wreath as you see here, with a needle case, an embroidery hoop, a tape measure, and some skeins of English crewel wool.

firmly and as close to each end as possible. Shape into a circle and, holding all six loose ends, match up the fabrics and temporarily pin together, so that each tube becomes one continuous piece.

One at a time, fold in the raw edges and oversew the ends together. Add extra batting so the seam is as full as the rest of the wreath.

Now comes the fun. Cover the seams by attaching your collection of gifts. Sew them in place with monofilament or tie them on with ribbons.

MATERIALS

3 cotton fabrics in assorted calico prints
Loose batting

ORDER OF WORKING

Cut each of the 3 fabrics into strips on the bias—one strip measuring 6" x 65". Double over each strip lengthwise and with right sides facing, machine-sew to make a long tube, leaving a ⅜" seam allowance. Turn right sides out and stuff with loose batting, forming three snake-like tubes.

Pin the three ends together, braid tightly and

66

CANDLE WREATH CENTERPIECE

(See photo page 67)

By adding quilted holly leaves and berries to a single tube of calico as used in the Gift Wreath (page 66), you can encircle a candle and create a centerpiece for your table.

MATERIALS

Cotton fabrics in assorted calicos, solids, and ginghams
¼" seam binding in coordinating colors
Batting, in sheets
Quilting thread

ORDER OF WORKING

Baste together like a sandwich two half-yard pieces of cotton fabric with batting in between. Cut whole leaf shapes in paper from the half-pattern shown below and arrange them as economically as possible on your sandwich of fabric. Outline the leaves with a Trace-Erase marker, and draw veins down the center of each as shown. Quilt the veins of the leaves through all 3 layers (see page 159). When all the quilting is complete, cut out the shapes and finish the raw edges with prefolded seam binding. For holly berries, cut circles 2" in diameter, following the technique for yo-yo's on page 72, and stuff each one with a little batting. Make a single tube of calico as described on page 66 and with monofilament thread, attach leaves and berries to cover it.

KISSENBAUM

(Color Plate 3 and photo opposite)

One of the things I loved about Christmas in England was our tradition of hanging a Kissenbaum in the archway outside our front door in London. The idea comes from Germany and Scandinavia, where they hang a circle of green pine, holly, and candles, and suspend apples and mistletoe in the center of the ring with long ribbons. Using the twisted braid base of the "Gift Wreath" (pages 66–67), you can add ribbons, felt berries, calico leaves, and electric candles, with their holders tucked between twists of the braids. Make a sprig of mistletoe and hang it from red ribbons with the apples in the center. Follow instructions for the wreath (page 66) Insert candles between the twists and wrap the wreath with ribbons, as in the photo. Make the mistletoe and berries in the same way as the holly leaves and berries on this page. The mistletoe berries will be just the right shade if you make the yo-yo circles in white organdy and stuff with yellow felt. Three lengths of fishing line (or monofilament) or green ribbons can be used to suspend the wreath from the ceiling. Red ribbons hang from the center to hold the apples and mistletoe. Sew the ribbons to the apples with buttonhole twist, pulling the thread right through the center of the apple, having made a hole with a skewer.

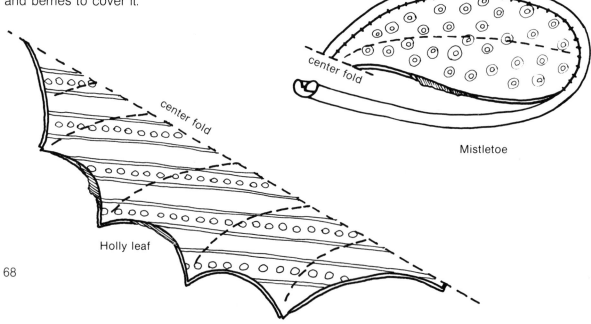

Mistletoe

Holly leaf

center fold

center fold

CHRISTMAS PLACEMATS

You can make your Christmas table really special with Santa's-stocking placemats. I chose a red-and-white-flowered cotton print to make the stocking, edged it with white eyelet lace, and tied it with a green ribbon. Then the prequilted mat and white napkin can be edged with a binding of the same color. You can tuck napkin, knife and fork, and gifts or candy canes into the stocking.

MATERIALS (measurements for 4 mats)

36″ wide calico or gaily patterned cotton
    fabric, 1¼ yards
36″ wide prequilted fabric, 1 yard
Frilled white eyelet edging, 1 yard
Ribbon, 2½ yards

ORDER OF WORKING

Cut out mats, oval as shown here or rectangular measuring 14″ top to bottom and 19″ from side to side. Cut binding (see page 159 for cutting continuous bias) and stitch around mat, right sides facing. Then turn to reverse side and hem.

Cut out stocking from the shape shown, plus ⅝″ turnbacks. Baste turnbacks, snipping the seam allowances to make smooth curves.

Machine-stitch eyelet and ribbon in place.

Hem stocking in position on mat.

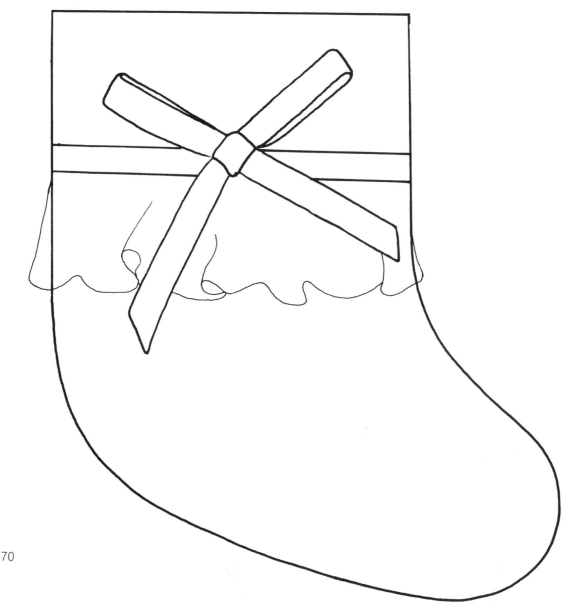

YO-YO WREATH AND ORNAMENT

The old familiar quilting techniques from grand-mother's day have found an up-to-date application for a wreath or an ornament. The wreath is made from rows of green, red, and red-and-white calico "yo-yo's"—fabric gathered in flat circles. The ornament is made from padded yo-yo's (inset) strung together to make a circle.

MATERIALS

100% cotton (easier to handle), gingham, or chintz fabrics—5 different colors (medium green, red, pale pink, dark green, and white) and approximately 1 yard each

4" round cardboard template (this gives a 2" yo-yo)

Cardboard for backing, cut in a "doughnut" shape 15" in diameter, 4" in width

Yo-yo's for the ornament (same size; 12 of them are strung together to form a circle, alternating red and green calicos)

ORDER OF WORKING

MAKING YO-YO'S

Circles call for extreme accuracy. If each one is not exactly the same size, joining them will be very difficult. Start by making a template, or brown paper pattern, double the size you want your finished circle to be. With curved scissors for smoothness, cut out your fabric ¼" larger than your paper pattern. Press down the turnbacks over the paper and work a row of running stitches close to the edge. Remove the pattern, draw it up tightly, press flat, and you have your first yo-yo. If you want to follow the coloring of the wreath shown here, you will need 5 different-colored fabrics. Make 23 of the shade you choose for the outside of the wreath, 22 of the next shade, 20, 15, and finally 12 of the inner ring color. Join them into strips, and sew them together.

ASSEMBLY

Cut out a "doughnut" in cardboard measuring 15" in diameter and with an 11" center opening. Cut out another doughnut in fabric the same size, adding 2" turnbacks on both sides. Place loose batting evenly on the cardboard and cover with the fabric. Snip and notch turnbacks and secure to back of cardborad with masking tape. Finish back by hemming another doughnut of fabric in place. Sew yo-yo's together in strips according to color. Beginning on the outside, tack the first row down, half extending beyond the backing. Tack down each of the next 4 rows, each one overlapping the preceding one. Attach a large bow made from one of the fabrics and decorate with pine cones or candy canes.

WOODLAND ANIMALS

Bring all the animals from the woods into the house this Christmas! You can make a wreath or a Christmas-tree skirt from this design, tracing it exactly as it is or enlarging it and adding your own favorites—blue jays, woodchucks, rabbits, and chipmunks, for instance. If the tree skirt is worked with the pine-branch pattern shown here, individual animals can also be made as matching ornaments. Then it will appear as if you carried the tree into the house complete with all the animals attached.

MATERIALS

White linen or polyester/cotton homespun
Red felt for backing wreath or Christmas-tree skirt
White felt for face of ornaments, green felt for backing
Dacron batting
Crewel wool
Natural-colored cotton floss for quilting

ORDER OF WORKING

Transfer the design from the drawings on these pages. The wreath is life-size and the skirt should be enlarged to fit under your tree. Work the design in one strand of Persian yarn, using straight stitch (page 156) for the pine needles, long and short and satin stitch (pages 25, 156) for the pine cones and animals, and open chain and herringbone stitches (opposite page) for the bow. When the wreath is complete, cut around the shape as in the photo on page 74, leaving ¾" seam allowance. Baste the turn-backs and pin and baste the design down onto a square of red felt. Pad with loose batting and stitch in place with quilting stitching (page 159) around the animals, and backstitch (page 156) along the outside edges in natural cotton floss. Cut out the red felt, leaving a border of approximately ¼" beyond the edge. Work the animal ornaments or the tree skirt in the same way, but instead of using backstitches at the edges, work a line of chain stitch in red or green around the circle ¼" in from the edge.

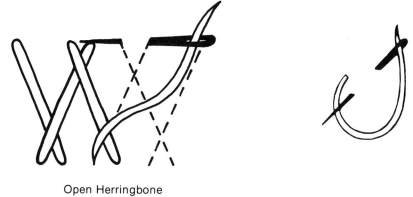

Open Herringbone

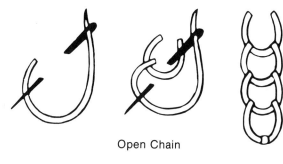

Open Chain

SILVER CANDELABRUM

(Color Plate 6)

Angels holding lamps, a mirrored flower, and a scrolled vase glittering in couched silver threads make a candelabrum for all seasons. The mirror is attached with Shisha work, a technique discovered by nomadic tribespeople in India, and the method of couching cords and padding leaves and petals probably originated in China; so the secrets of the Orient will be stitched into your international needlework. The best-kept secret of all is what you use for your padding—felt and heavy waxed string. No one would know, looking at the elegant finished piece, that such humble materials were used underneath.

MATERIALS

A. Medium silver cord
B. Heavy silver cord
C. Lumi yarn
D. Fil d'argent DMC
E. Broad silver ribbon
F. Japanese silver
G. Stardust lamé
H. Narrow silver ribbon
J. Camelot silver thread

Metal threads: see Suppliers.

Horsetail or gray maltese sewing silk
Packaging twine or string
White linen twill
Metal- or glass-encased night lights
Wood or fiberboard base
Mirror—⅛" thick, 3" diameter (flat, thin makeup mirror)

ORDER OF WORKING

(1) Enlarge the pattern on page 82 to measure 21½" high. (2) Mount the fabric in a square embroidery frame of artist's stretcher strips. (3) Using 4 strands of gray cotton floss, hold the mirror in place in the center (step 1 of Shisha stitch). Using pliable Camelot silver thread, work Shisha stitch around the mirror (steps 2–7). (4) Work all crewel stitches, such as herringbone stitch, French knots, satin stitch, and plain couching. The pattern indicates the stitch and the letter indicates which thread to use.

80

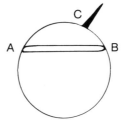

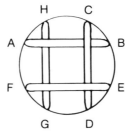

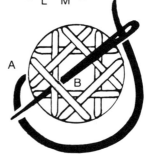

Shisha Stitch

1. Place mirror in position and hold in place. Come up at A and down at B, close to edges, to make a horizontal stitch one-third down from top of mirror. Come up at C, one third in from B.

2. Continue around mirror, from C to D, E to F, G to H, making a square as shown.

3. Repeat around mirror, following the letters, to make a diamond on top of the square as shown. These "holding" stitches keep the mirror firm.

4. Using a blunt needle, come up at A. Slide needle under the holding stitches, and with thread under needle, draw tight.

5. Take a small stitch into the fabric, close to the edge, from C to D and with thread under needle, draw tight.

6. Repeat 4, sliding needle under the holding threads, and draw tight with the thread under the needle.

7. Repeat 5, but go down into the same hole at D *inside* the loop. Come up at F with thread under needle.

8. Continue, repeating steps 6 and 7 to make a close band of stitching around mirror, catching in all the holding stitches so that they are completely concealed.

close herringbone

couching over string

French knots

satin stitch over felt

satin stitch

couching over felt

flat couching

ribbon couching over string

82

PADDING WITH FELT. Pad with felt all raised areas that are marked, couching over felt or satin stitch over felt. Starting with the central flower petals, pad each one in the following way: trace a paper pattern of the first petal and cut it out in felt. Cut a second shape slightly smaller, and a third one smaller still. Stitch them lightly into position on your design with the largest on top. Now, couch Japanese silver thread to completely cover the felt on each petal following the instructions below. Repeat the procedure for all areas marked couching over felt. All the felt padding is done in the same way whether it is covered with couching or satin stitch as indicated in the graph. Work the satin stitch over felt in one strand of Fil d'argent following the directional lines on the chart.

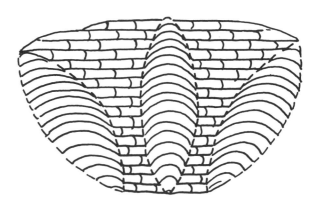

Contour Couching over Felt

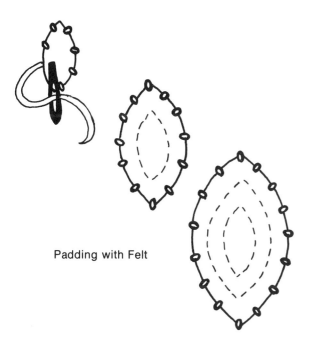

Padding with Felt

Satin Stitch over Felt

Straight Couching over Felt

PADDING WITH STRING. Areas marked with a wavy line on the chart are padded with string. Sew down the string as in the diagram "Couching Flowers over String," and couch 2 strands of Japanese silver over it, placing the couching stitch to one side of the string. Work the top of the vase in ribbon couched over string (see diagram on page 85).

83

MOUNTING

The finished embroidery should be mounted on a ½" plywood or fiberboard in a rectangle or in the shape shown in the photograph. First, cover the board with a layer of foam rubber or thin batting, then tape embroidery firmly over it. Also in plywood, cut out 4 ledges to support the candles in the shape shown in the diagram. Cover each ledge with fabric, and glue a silver braid around the edge to cover the front edge seams. With a drill, make 2 small holes for each ledge, above the angels, in the same position indicated on the graph, making sure that the lower candles are clear of the upper ones so the ledges do not burn. Next, to hold ledges in place, first mark holes by poking a needle or skewer through the holes in the backing. Drill two small holes into each ledge and, from the back, screw them into position.

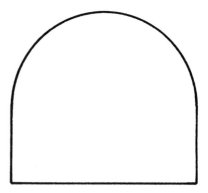

Candelabrum Ledge

Couching to Fill a Shape

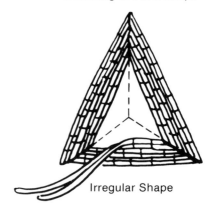

Irregular Shape

Couching at Corners

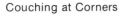

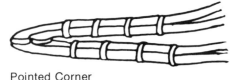

Pointed Corner

Start at outer edge, working around and around to the center, "bricking" the couching stitches as shown. At each corner, sew over each silver thread separately at the angle of the shape shown.

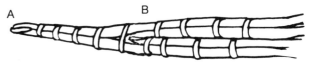

Long Narrow Shape

Squared Corner

When a shape is very thin and tapered, take only one of the pair of threads to the outer limit of the shape (at A). Secure it with a double stitch for firmness at the point and double it back on itself, couching it back to meet the second thread (at B). Turn the thread at B back sharply, secure with a double stitch, and continue couching them both together, as the shape widens.

Each thread is sewn separately at the point.

84

Couching "Flowers" over String

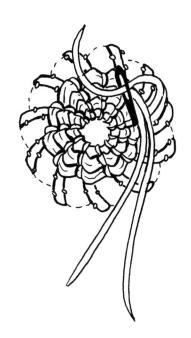

Draw a circle with lines radiating from center. Sew string down over lines as shown. Fold a strand of Japanese silver in half and sew loop end down at center of flower. Work from center out, sewing the 2 strands together and placing a couching stitch to one side of the string as shown. Completely cover the string without crowding rows.

Couching Ribbon over String

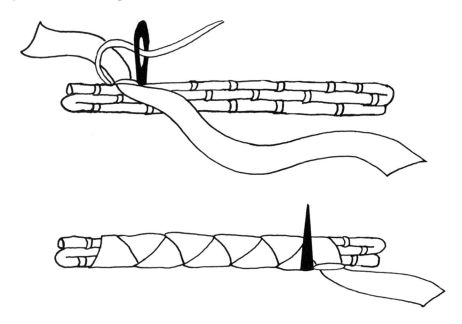

Couch over single strands of string laid side by side to form the desired thickness. Place ribbons along edge of string; take a double stitch over the ribbon close to and parallel with the string. Fold the ribbon over the string and repeat this double stitch on the other side. Continue in this manner, crisscrossing the string base with ribbon until it is covered completely.

AUTUMN LEAVES TABLECLOTH

A ring of autumn leaves and berries, red toadstools, and green pine branches makes a festive Christmas cloth that you can use all year round. White Dacron and cotton batiste is a sheer background fabric perfect for showing off the colors (or natural linen, as you see here), and the stitches can be simple split and satin stitch to give the cotton floss the look of enamel.

MATERIALS

1½ yards cotton/Dacron broadcloth or sheer batiste (Dacron plus cotton allows it to wash well and drip dry with little ironing), or 54″ wide natural linen for a hard-wearing, long-lasting tablecloth
6-strand cotton floss (use 3 or 4 strands)
Trace-Erase marker (see Suppliers)

ORDER OF WORKING

Fold fabric in four; crease well, and trim to make a perfect square. Double over a ⅝″ hem on all four sides, and use Point de Paris (page 158) as a decorative hemstitch. Now look at the diagram on page 88 for placing the design. From the center of the cloth (marked by the crease lines), draw a circle with a radius of 4″; then draw a circle outside this with a radius of 10″. (If you use a Trace-Erase marker, you can eliminate unwanted lines afterward by simply touching with cold water.) Trace the full-size design on page 89 (one-quarter is shown) between the circles and repeat it to form a ring, matching A to B as shown on the design placement chart. Using 3 threads of cotton floss, work all the leaves in split stitch, berries in satin stitch, and ferns in fishbone stitch (see page 156 for stitches). Be careful about beginning and ending stitches—do not "jump" from one shape to another, as the thread will show through the sheer fabric.

When finished, press the wrong side into a thick blanket, using a steam iron or a damp cloth.

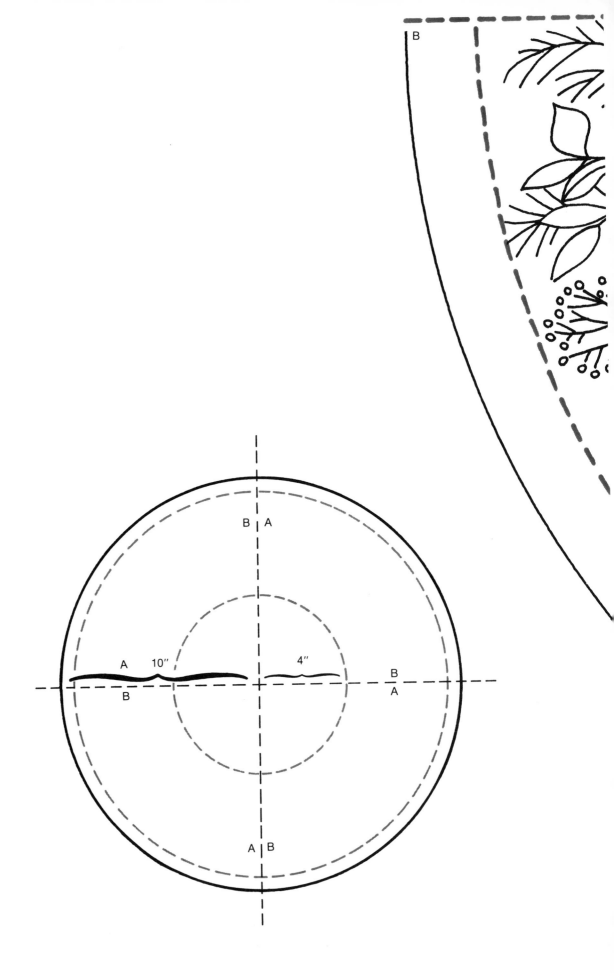

A

CROSS-STITCH HAND TOWELS

Small cross-stitch motifs are ready to be worked so that even the bathroom is ready for Christmas! Remember, of course, that the repeat patterns would also be excellent for table linen. You can simply count them from the graphs on this page and use them any way you wish—for placemats, an apron, a rug—perhaps even as a Christmas card.

MATERIALS

14-to-the-inch Aida cloth, off white
Cotton embroidery floss in colors shown on
  graph

ORDER OF WORKING

For a finished size of 12″ x 20″, cut hand towels 13″ x 24½″.

Draw out a thread at top and bottom 3″ in from the edge. Fold over 1″ and 1″ again and hemstitch (page 157).

Find the center point in the width and count up 16 threads from the hemstitching. On thread 17, begin counting out the pattern from the graph, using 2 threads of cotton floss. Christmas trees are spaced 12 threads apart at bottom row.

Finish the sides by folding over a double turnback ¼″ wide, and hemming.

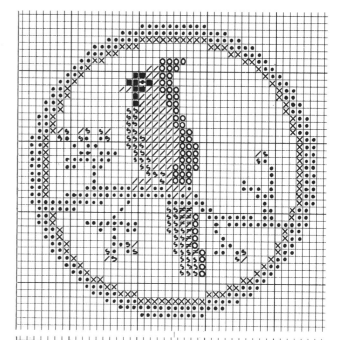

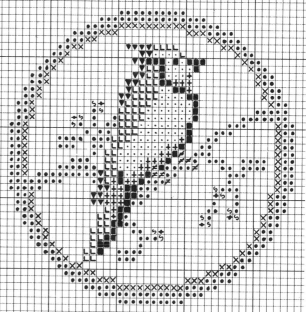

	medium red
	light red
	dark green
	dark red
	medium gray
	medium blue
	light green
	black
	light blue
	light gray
	dark brown

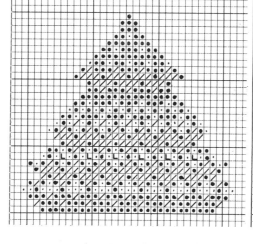

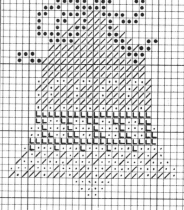

QUILTED NATIVITY SCENE
(Color Plate 8)

*"Sing joy for the children
Come Christmas morn,
Little Christ Jesus
Our brother is born."*

A triptych that can stand on the mantelpiece can be made of appliqué like a collage, combining it with embroidery stitches and quilting. The angels can peek out from behind the clouds, and all the figures can be attached to the background with Velcro.

MATERIALS

100% cotton fabric in assorted colors
Cotton floss
Velcro or snappers
Cardboard
Batting

ORDER OF WORKING

FIGURES

(1) Transfer the patterns on pages 97–99 to paper. (2) Choose a piece of fabric in the basic color of the figure, large enough to fit into a hoop. Trace the entire figure onto the cloth with Trace-Erase or light pencil. (3) Cut face shapes with ¼" turnbacks from flesh-colored fabric and appliqué in place, clipping and folding under turnbacks. Cut legs and candle glow from the blue and yellow fabrics, and appliqué in place to kneeling figures. Cut white blanket and halo and brown manger and appliqué to Jesus figure. (4) With cotton floss, embroider all details—hair, halos, eyes, hands, shoes, and manger straw. (5) Cut out figures, leaving a ½" turnback all around. Cut a second piece of fabric in the same color for a backing. (6) With right sides together stitch around ½" from outer edge, leaving an opening. (7) Clip turnbacks and turn right side out. (8) Stuff lightly with batting and slip-stitch opening closed. (9) Quilt figures along dotted lines shown. (10) Sew small pieces of Velcro or snappers to the backs and in position on triptych.

TREES

(1) Trace patterns to green fabric. (2) Cut out fronts and matching backs, allowing for ½" turnbacks. (3) With right sides together, seam ½" from edge leaving opening. (4) Clip turnbacks, turn right side out and stuff. (5) Slip-stitch opening closed. (6) Quilt along dotted lines and sew Velcro or snappers to back of trees and in position on triptych.

TRIPTYCH AND CLOUDS

(1) Using methods described on page 153, enlarge triptych patterns to the size indicated by diagram (page 96). (2) Make paper patterns of enlarged clouds in the shapes diagramed on pages 94-96. (3) For blue-edged clouds, trace central sections of clouds on white or dark blue fabric as indicated by color key. (4) Cut a front only, allowing ½" turnback. (5) For light blue edging, trace outline of entire cloud onto fabric large enough for hoop. (6) Appliqué white or dark blue center sections to cloth around outside edge. (7) Stuff lightly and quilt along dotted lines. (8) Cut out blue cloud shapes, allowing for ½" turnbacks. Cut out matching shape for back. (9) Seam as for trees, leaving open edge at bottom. (10) Turn and stuff lightly along blue outline area of the top edge. Quilt blue edge just above white cloud to hold stuffing in place. (11) Following the layouts, tack clouds to each other, allowing for "pockets" to hold angels.

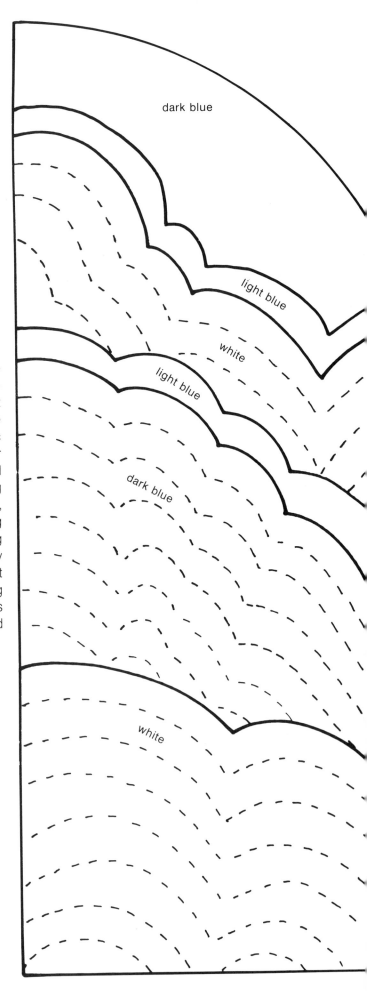

94

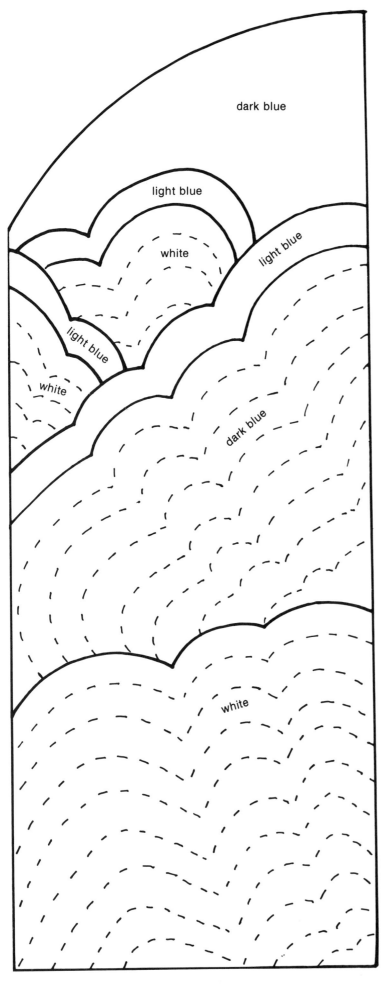

dark blue

light blue

white

light blue

light blue

white

white

dark blue

white

FINISHING

(1) Use enlarged pattern pieces to cut 3 cardboard sections for triptych base. (2) Cover both sides with dark blue fabric, leaving bottom open on front. (3) Lightly stuff front side and slip-stitch the edge closed. (4) Appliqué moon to left side. (5) Position cloud sections to cardboard base, fold under turnbacks, and whip-stitch in place. (Make sure that cloud edges line up properly when the 3 sides are joined together.) (6) Position figures and trees as desired. Sew Velcro pieces to background and attach figures. Place angels in cloud "pockets." (7) With loose but firm stitches, sew side panels to center of triptych, so sides will be flexible.

Triptych finished size

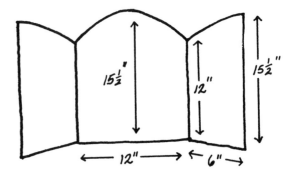

$15\frac{1}{2}$"   12" $15\frac{1}{2}$"

12"   6"

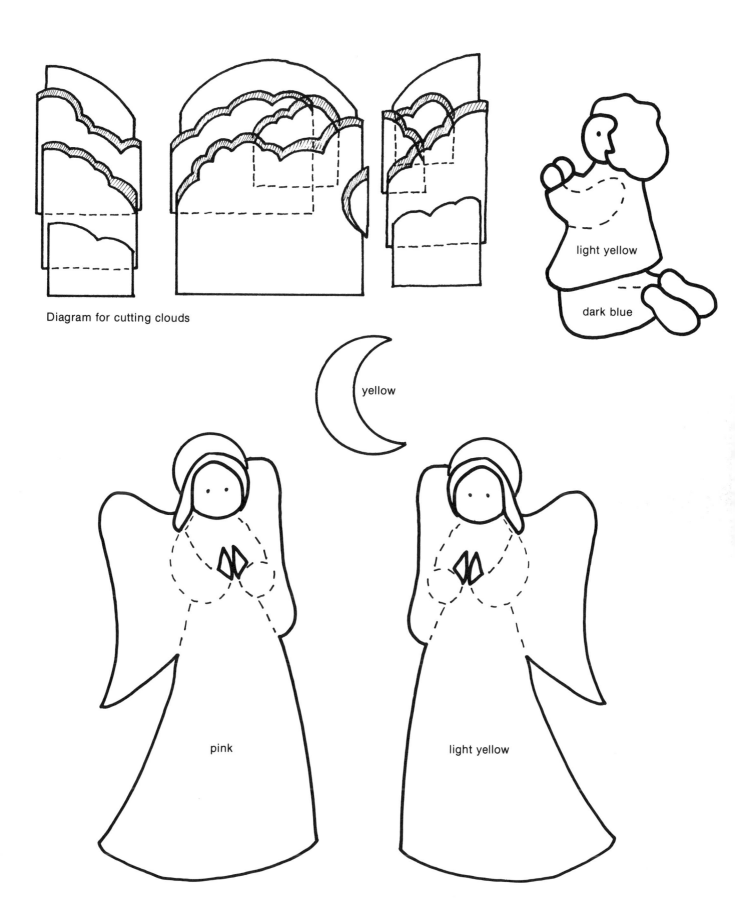

Diagram for cutting clouds

light yellow

dark blue

yellow

pink

light yellow

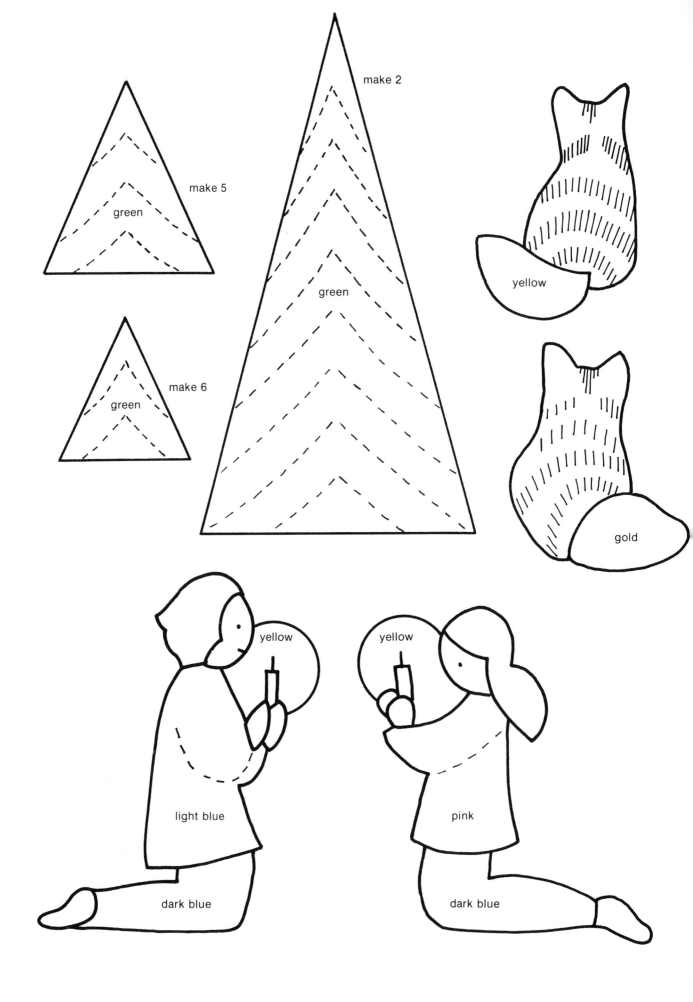

make 5

green

make 6

green

make 2

green

yellow

gold

yellow

yellow

light blue

pink

dark blue

dark blue

yellow

white

brown

light yellow

green

pink

A CHRISTMAS SAMPLER

Here are the symbols of Christmas, all worked into one sampler with silver and gold metal thread and fine cotton floss on sheer white cotton/Dacron batiste. Work it in one simple flat stitch to accentuate the delicacy of the thread and background material. Take care that all your threads are neatly concealed as you begin and end off, and never "jump" across the back from one area to another. Then the sampler can be mounted and hung in a window like stained glass, or framed in a shadow box as a lighted panel. Alternatively, since this is a sampler, use it in the original meaning of the word—as a reference guide—and scatter the motifs on a tablecloth or a runner.

MATERIALS

Panel measures 12" x 17"
Sheer cotton/Dacron batiste
Cotton floss
Fil d'or gold metal thread (DMC)
Fil d'argent silver thread (DMC)

ORDER OF WORKING

Trace the designs, shown in full scale on the next pages, onto your fabric, arranging them as they are shown opposite, or making your own composition. If you are using sheer material, you can trace them directly, using a hard (H) pencil. Using only one thread of cotton floss, work long and short stitches in all large areas. Work satin stitch in smaller ones. Work stitches only around edges of Christmas rose and leave the center open to show French knots on stalks. Use one thread for all satin stitching in Fil d'or and Fil d'argent metal thread. Outline each motif in chain stitch, and backstitch all the lettering.

MOUNTING

Stretch on artist's stretcher strips, using the *outside* measurement of the strips, so that the panel is clear. Back the stretchers with a shadow box, so that the panel will stand away from the wall. Tape small white Christmas lights to the back of the design, behind the stretchers. Lightly glue ribbon to the front of the stretchers to cover the area where the wood shows through the fabric. The design will look its best when some light comes from the back and the front at the same time.

Rosemary

poinsetta

Flower of the Holy Night

Mistletoe

golden bough of peace

Behold I bring you

Balthasar
Melchior
Gaspar

good tidings
of great joy

Three Wise Men

Myrrh-death

holly
symbol of
the crown of thorns

frankincense

worship

gold - tribute

...the Spirit of God descending

like a dove...

The Star of Bethlehem

The Christmas Rose

THE NIGHT BEFORE CHRISTMAS

'Twas the night before Christmas
And all through the house,
Not a creature was stirring,
Not even a mouse. . . .

Well, Chessie, the mascot of the famous railroad of the same name, is sleeping as soundly as a kitten should, but Beatrix Potter's mouse from her Christmas story about the Tailor of Gloucester was actually up all night stitching the mayor's embroidered coat, to help the poor tailor who was sick in bed. You could hang these two pillows on the door as you pretend to be Santa and fill the stockings, or they would make adorable gifts to send instead of a Christmas card. Chessie is all ready for the great day with a little silver bell and a red ribbon, and the Tailor of Gloucester's mouse has a real silver needle in her hand. Both pillows are edged and backed with bright red velvet.

MATERIALS

Linen
Cotton floss
Muslin
Dacron padding
Red velvet for backing
Piping cord
Silver metal thread, needle, silver bell

ORDER OF WORKING

Trace the life-size designs shown on the following pages. Using 3 strands of embroidery floss, begin with Chessie's head in long and short stitch. Start at the top of the head and work stripes of black and light gray, blending them into dark gray. Work the area above the nose in tan. The area around the eye and mouth is worked in white, shading to tan and ecru. Work the eyes and mouth in black straight stitch, the nose in pink satin stitch. Next, work the paw in long and short stitch, blending dark gray and light gray. Chessie's sheets are backstitched in Camelot silver, then underlined in pale blue floss. The lettering is backstitched red. Finally, work the ribbon in bright red satin stitch, and sew the silver bell in the center of the bow.

Work the mouse in long and short stitch, blending ecru, tan, light brown, and medium brown, following the body contour. Work the eyes in black satin stitch with the pupil in white on top, the whiskers in black straight stitch, and the tail in tan satin stitch.

The mouse's embroidery is worked in lazy-daisy flowers with French knot centers of pale pink, medium pink, and medium blue on a ground of olive green stem stitch and grass green lazy-daisy leaves. The lettering is in red backstitch, and the thread is medium pink stem stitch. When the embroidery is finished, attach a needle threaded with medium pink, holding it in place by satin-stitching the mouse's paw over it. (For stitches, see pages 111, 156, 157).

...not a creature was stirring...

not even a mouse

To mount the door pillow cut a piece of velvet 1″ x 30″, and fold it in half lengthwise, inserting a heavy cord in the fold. Baste together close to the cord to form the piping. Baste the piping to the right side of the pillow, raw edges toward the outside, and join the ends together at the bottom of the door pillow.

For the handle cut a strip of velvet 10″ x 1½″, and fold under turnbacks of ½″ along long edges. Fold strip in half lengthwise around a cord. Machine-stitch close to the cord, about ⅛″ from open side. Attach the ends of the handle to the top of the door pillow 1½″ in from the corners. Cut a piece of velvet for the backing, allowing ⅝″ all around for seam allowance. With right sides facing, pin the front and back together. Baste together, making sure the piping is ¼″ inside the basting line. Machine-stitch along the basting line, leaving a 3″ opening at the bottom. Trim seam allowance, clip corners, and turn right side out. Stuff with fiberfill and slip-stitch the opening closed.

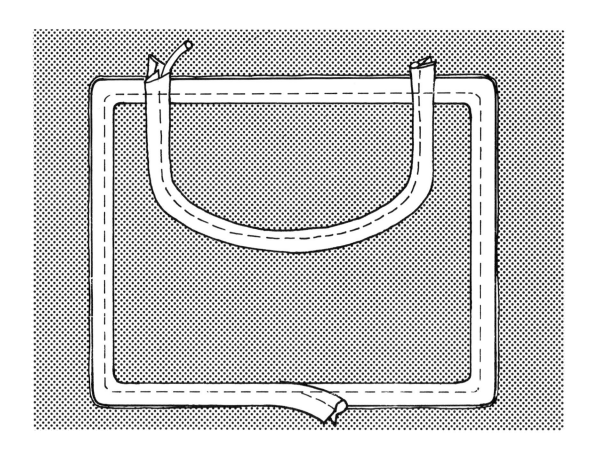

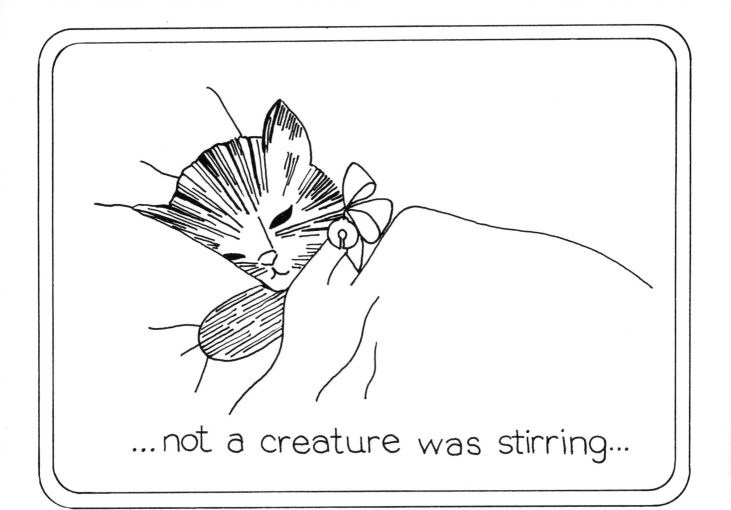

...not a creature was stirring...

...not even a mouse

'TIS THE SEASON TO BE JOLLY

What would Christmas be without children?! On the following pages are things not only to entertain children but possibly for them to make. There are cuddly toys that they may love and cherish long after they are too grown up to play with them, and there are simple ornaments that the youngest child will enjoy making with nimble fingers and keen eyesight. Others are things you can make *for* children. A baby's bib, the ideal gift for the youngest member of the family at Christmas, and a Beatrix Potter Christmas tree, from a sketch by the author of the most enchanting animal books for children of every age.

BEATRIX POTTER CHRISTMAS PICTURE

What could be merrier than a band of Beatrix Potter animals dancing around the Christmas tree! This charming design will delight children and adults year after year. Enlarge it to 16″ x 20″ for a framed picture or use it the size shown (12″ x 17″) as a pillow.

MATERIALS

Fine-weave white linen or poly/cotton home-spun, ½ yard
Persian wool

ORDER OF WORKING

1. Transfer the life-size drawing according to instructions on page 153.
2. TREE: forest green, kelly green, and light green straight stitch
3. ORNAMENTS: light orange satin stitch
4. CANDLES: flame straight stitch
5. Animals around the tree, from left to right:
   MICE
   > face—light gray satin stitch
   > highlights and features—black straight stitch
   > tails—light gray stem stitch
   > song books—yellow straight stitch

   MOUSE CONDUCTOR
   > face—light brown satin stitch
   > eye and ear highlights—dark brown straight stitch
   > dress—medium blue chain stitch
   > collar—white satin stitch

   SQUIRRELS
   > bodies—light rust, medium rust long and short
   > bellies—white long and short
   > tail—peach long and short

   HEDGEHOG
   > head, hands, and legs—light and medium brown long and short
   > features—dark brown straight stitch
   > apron—white long and short, outline blue backstitch
   > dress—light apple green stem stitch

cap—white long and short
shoes—black satin stitch

MR. MOUSE
> head and body—medium brown long and short
> eye—dark brown French knot
> whiskers—outline dark brown backstitch
> vest—pale yellow long and short
> jacket—light apple green, apple green long and short
> shoes—black satin stitch

CAT
> head, body, tail—peach, medium rust, light brown long and short
> features—black straight stitch
> shoes—brown satin stitch
> bagpipes and cap—medium blue straight stitch
> pompon on hat—white cut turkey work

INSECTS
> bodies—dark brown long and short
> skirt (*left*)—red-orange chain stitch
> pants (*right*)—red-orange close herring-bone
> wing (*right*)—light apple green close her-ringbone

FROG
> body—light apple green, apple green long and short
> eyes—white satin stitch, outlines black backstitch

RABBITS IN FOREGROUND
> head and bodies—medium brown long and short
> eyes—dark brown French Knots
> outlines around head and ears—dark brown backstitch
> jackets—medium blue and dark blue long and short
> tails—white cut turkey work

RABBITS IN BACKGROUND
> heads—peach, light rust long and short
> eyes—dark brown French knots

outlines around ears—dark brown backstitch

SQUIRRELS
    heads—light rust, medium rust long and
      short
    highlights—dark brown backstitch
    eyes—dark brown straight stitch
    tails—peach straight stitch

JEMIMA PUDDLEDUCK
    body—white satin stitch
    beak—yellow satin stitch
    hat—medium blue, dark blue satin stitch
    eye—dark brown French knot

6 ANIMALS ON TREE
    squirrel—body and tail, peach, light rust,
      medium rust long and short
    eye—dark brown straight stitch

BIRD (top)
    body—red satin stitch
    eyes, beak, and claws—black straight
      stitch

BIRD
    body—red, yellow long and short
    beak, claws—black straight stitch
    eye—black French knot

6. LETTERING: orange stem stitch
7. STARS: yellow straight stitch

For shaded long and short stitching, work the
first row, as in the diagram, coming up at A and
going down at B, starting at the highest point of
each shape and fanning the stitches outward.
Work the second row of stitches in the next
shade lighter or darker, coming up at C and
splitting each stitch on the first row about one-
third of the way up. Work the third row, coming
up at E (splitting the stitches on the previous
row) and going down at F. There will be fewer
stitches on the third row since the space to be
filled is smaller than at the top.

For other stitches, see pages 46, 147, 150, 156,
157.

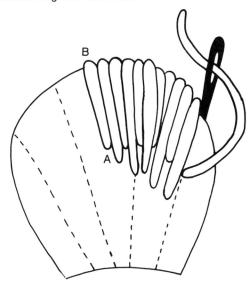

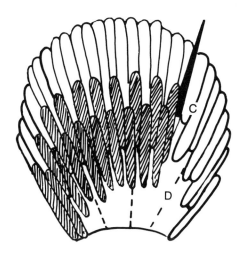

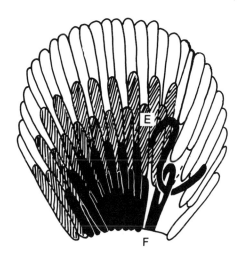

'tis the sea

on to be jolly

BEATRIX POTTER ANIMALS

(Color Plate 5)

Here are some of my favorite Beatrix Potter animals—Peter Rabbit on a stocking, and Jemima Puddleduck, Mrs. Tiggywinkle, and Benjamin Bunny, all painted on soft cotton, stitched and quilted, and padded to make soft toys. My son, Illya, and a neighboring cat posed for the photo opposite, and the patterns are on the following pages.

This is a great idea for anyone with a little skill at painting or crayoning. These soft toys can be made in almost any size, by painting with textile paints, adding embroidery touches, and padding. The Peter Rabbit stocking is first painted, then appliquéd and padded. A charming Christmas-tree skirt could be made in the same way, or an apron to wear at home at Christmastime.

MATERIALS

Prequilted cotton or polyester fabric, white
Cotton or polyester, unquilted
Loose batting
Quilting thread
Cotton embroidery thread
Prefolded bias seam binding
Fabric paints, Pentel crayons, liquid embroidery, permanent markers (see Suppliers)

ORDER OF WORKING

Enlarge the outlines on the following pages, trace them onto white soft cotton, and fill in the simple shapes with Pentel crayons. These are wax crayons that can be ironed on the reverse side; the heat sets the paint permanently. Alternatively, use fabric paints that are on the market and quite easy to handle (see Suppliers). Once the painting is complete, add embroidery touches, such as eyes and nose and buttonhole edgings around Mrs. Tiggywinkle's baby's blanket. Join back and front, right sides facing, turn inside out and stuff firmly. Sew up the opening.

PETER RABBIT STOCKING

Paint or crayon Peter Rabbit in the same way, allowing extra fabric around the edges to be taken up by the padding. Stay-stitch around the entire outline; this will hold the shape and pre-

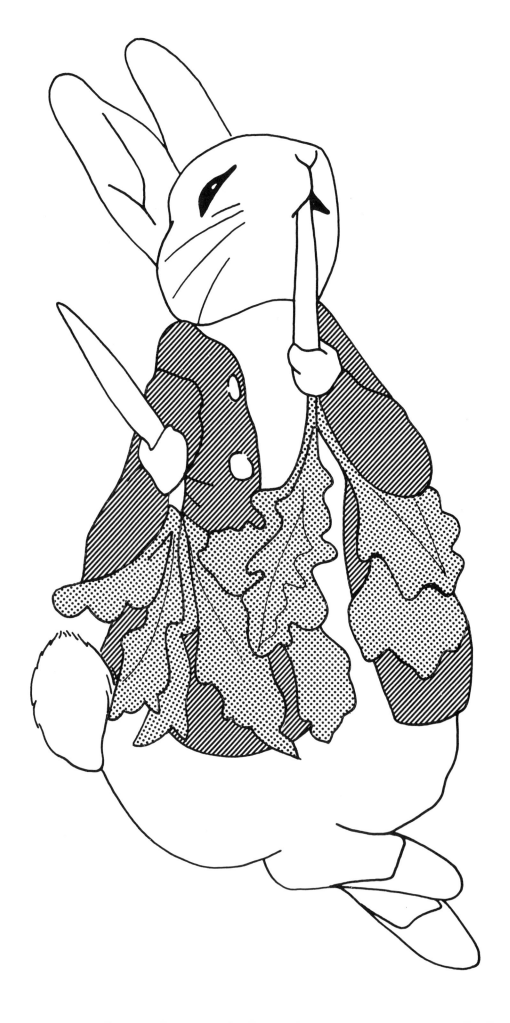

vent fraying when appliquéd. Cut out, leaving a ⅜" seam allowance all around. Baste the outline of a Christmas stocking onto the prequilted fabric, and center Peter on the stocking as shown in the photo. Turn back raw edges and begin to appliqué, stuffing each section as you sew it in place. Quilt around the large areas, such as the jacket, head, ears, carrots, and leaves.

When the entire design is appliquéd, stuffed, and quilted, work any lettering in stem stitch. Cut out the stocking and backing to the finished size; a seam allowance is not necessary. With the prefolded seam binding, cover the edges at the top of the stocking. Pin the front to the back and join together with seam binding around the stocking, leaving the top open. Leave a loop at the top for hanging.

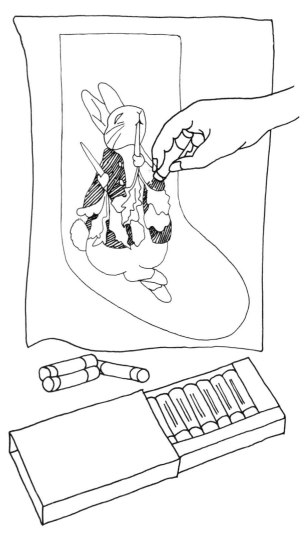

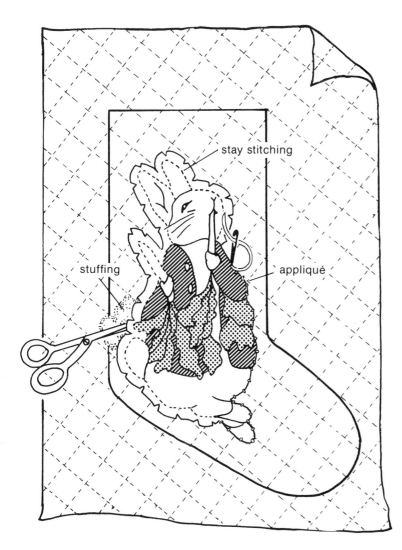

stay stitching

stuffing

appliqué

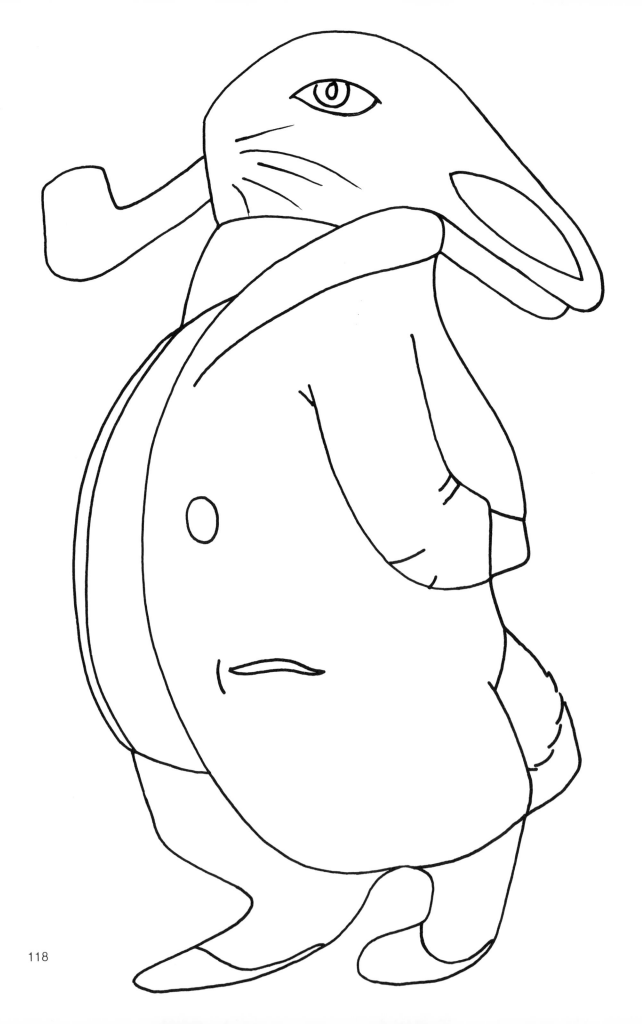

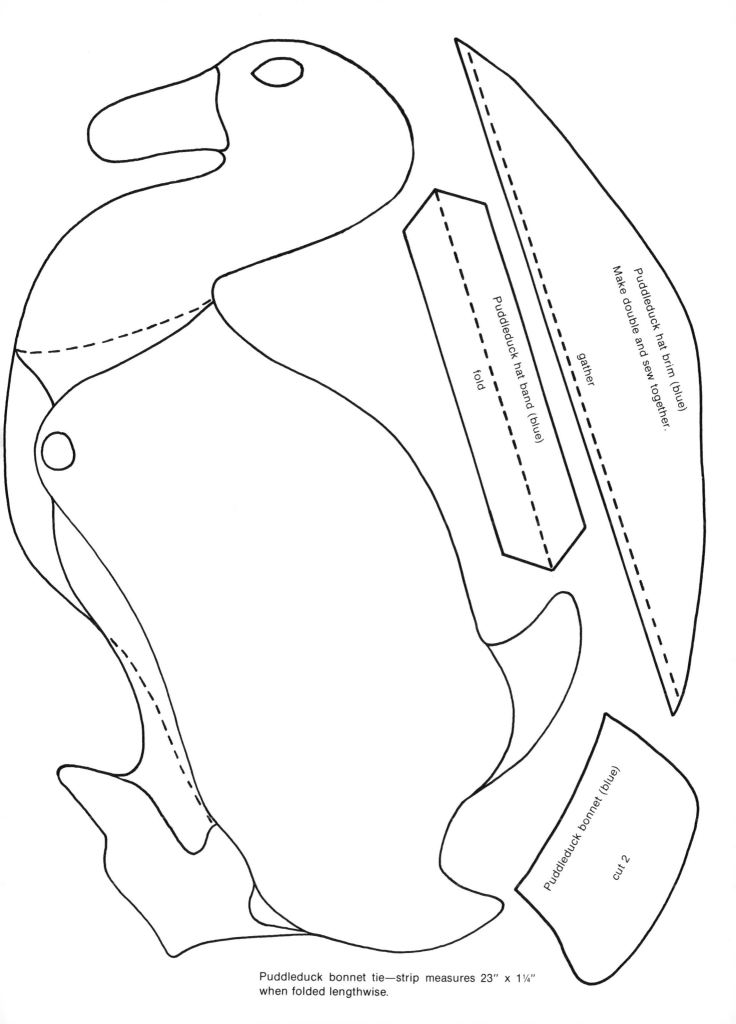

Puddleduck hat brim (blue)
Make double and sew together.

gather

Puddleduck hat band (blue)

fold

Puddleduck bonnet (blue)

cut 2

Puddleduck bonnet tie—strip measures 23″ x 1¼″ when folded lengthwise.

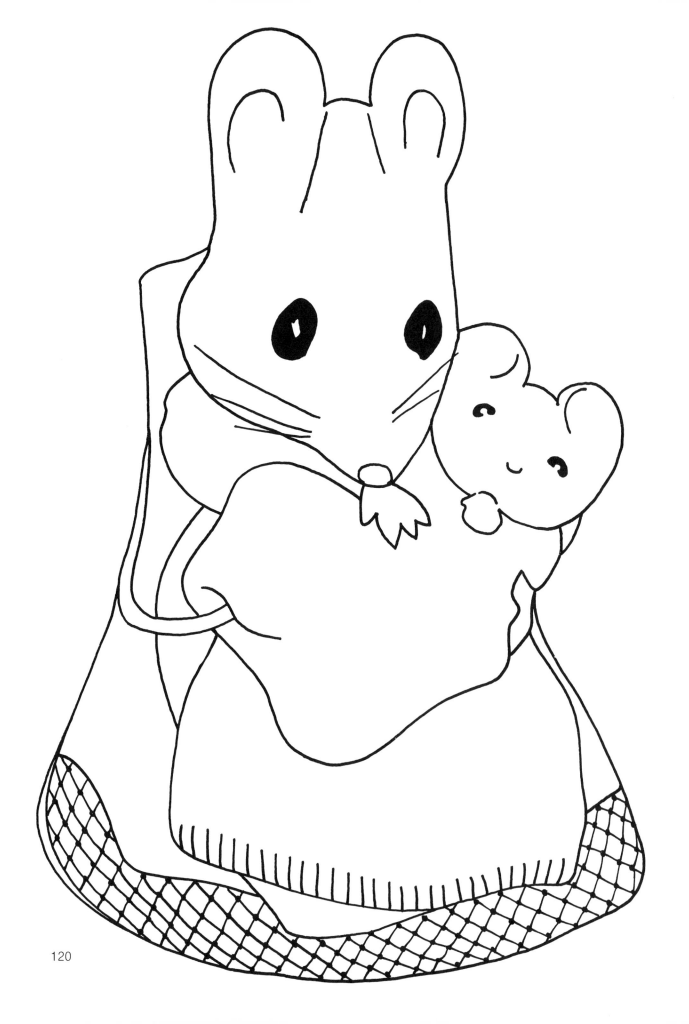

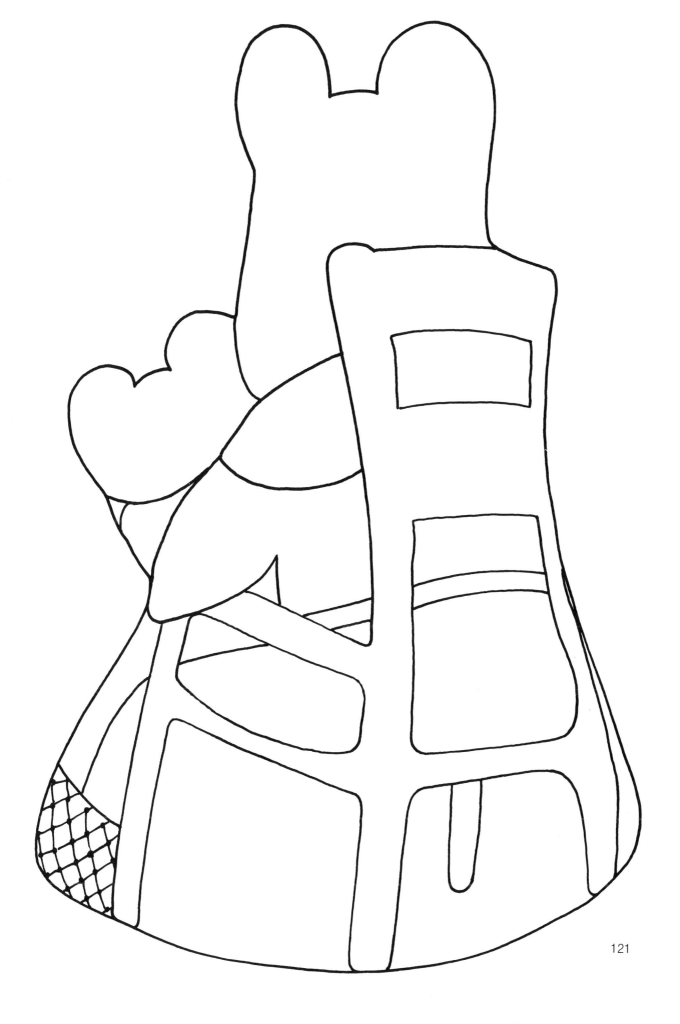

121

JEREMY FISHER

The amiable frog, Jeremy Fisher, from Beatrix Potter's story of that name, has a white felt waistcoat with embroidered flowers and a bright red coat. If you make him a bean-bag frog, he will settle easily into marvelously "froggy" positions, and you'll probably get carried away and start making a transparent plastic raincoat and a fishing creel in plastic canvas, or even a little packet of butterfly sandwiches to eat whilst he's waiting for that fish to jump!

MATERIALS

Felt and cardboard
Cotton embroidery floss
Loose batting or bean filling

COLORS

Waistcoat: white, pink, and green embroidery, red buttons
Coat: red
Body: green
Eyes: black, white, green
Mouth: red
Bands on legs: yellow
Feet: white
Shoes: black

ORDER OF WORKING

Cut out all the pieces using the patterns on the next pages. Start with the mouth. Fold a piece of scored cardboard in half and cover it inside with red felt. After joining all the body pieces, oversew the mouth in place and stuff lightly with loose batting (add bean filling only to the body, arms, and legs). For the eyes, gather a black circle of felt and pad it with a little cotton. Stitch around it a "collar" of doubled strips of white felt. Then stitch down an eyelid of green felt to half cover it, as in the photo. Sew strips of felt to flat leg shapes, then stitch legs in tubes and stuff them. Sew up the tops of both legs, attach them to the body, and stitch them together with long stitches, joining them inside the body to hold them firm. Repeat for the arms. Embroider the vest with lazy daisy stitches and French knot

buttons. Do up the vest and coat with oversewing stitches; no turnbacks are necessary with the felt. Complete the costume with a sheer batiste triangle or handkerchief tied at the neck.

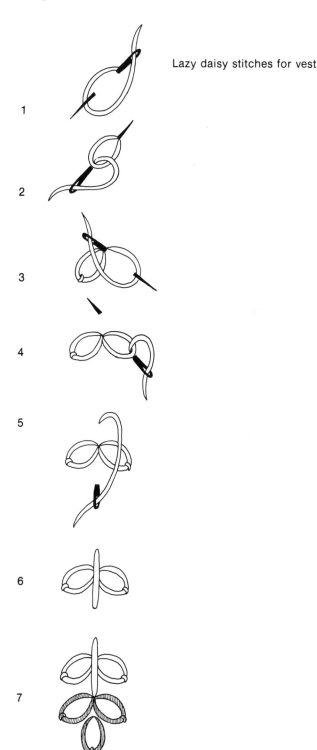

Lazy daisy stitches for vest

1
2
3
4
5
6
7

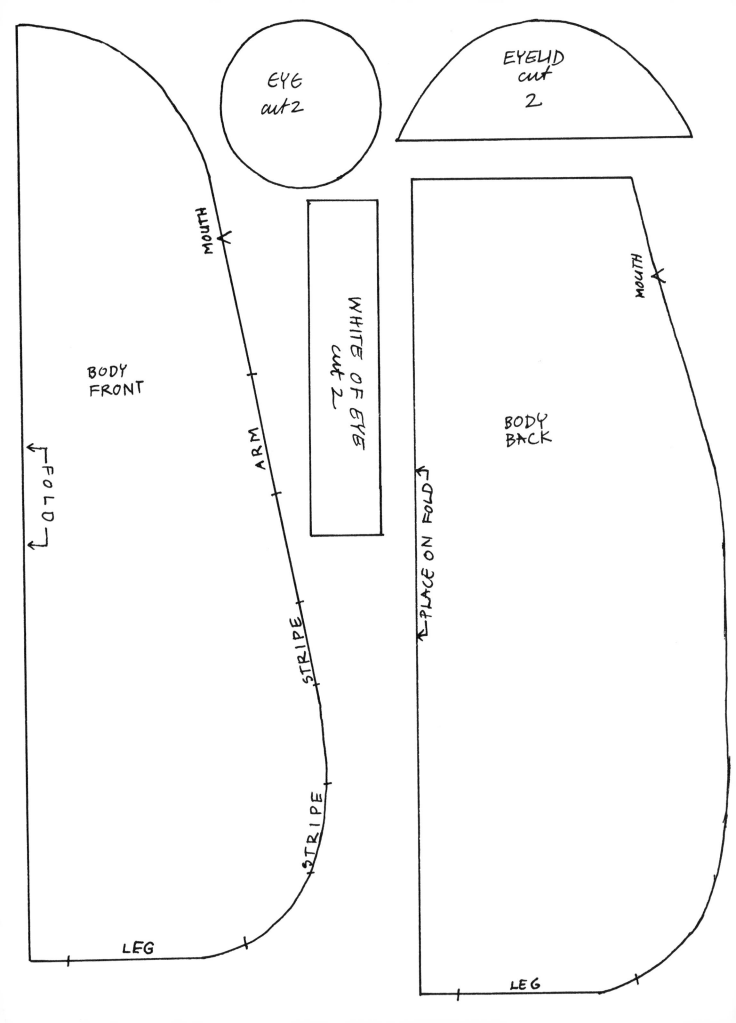

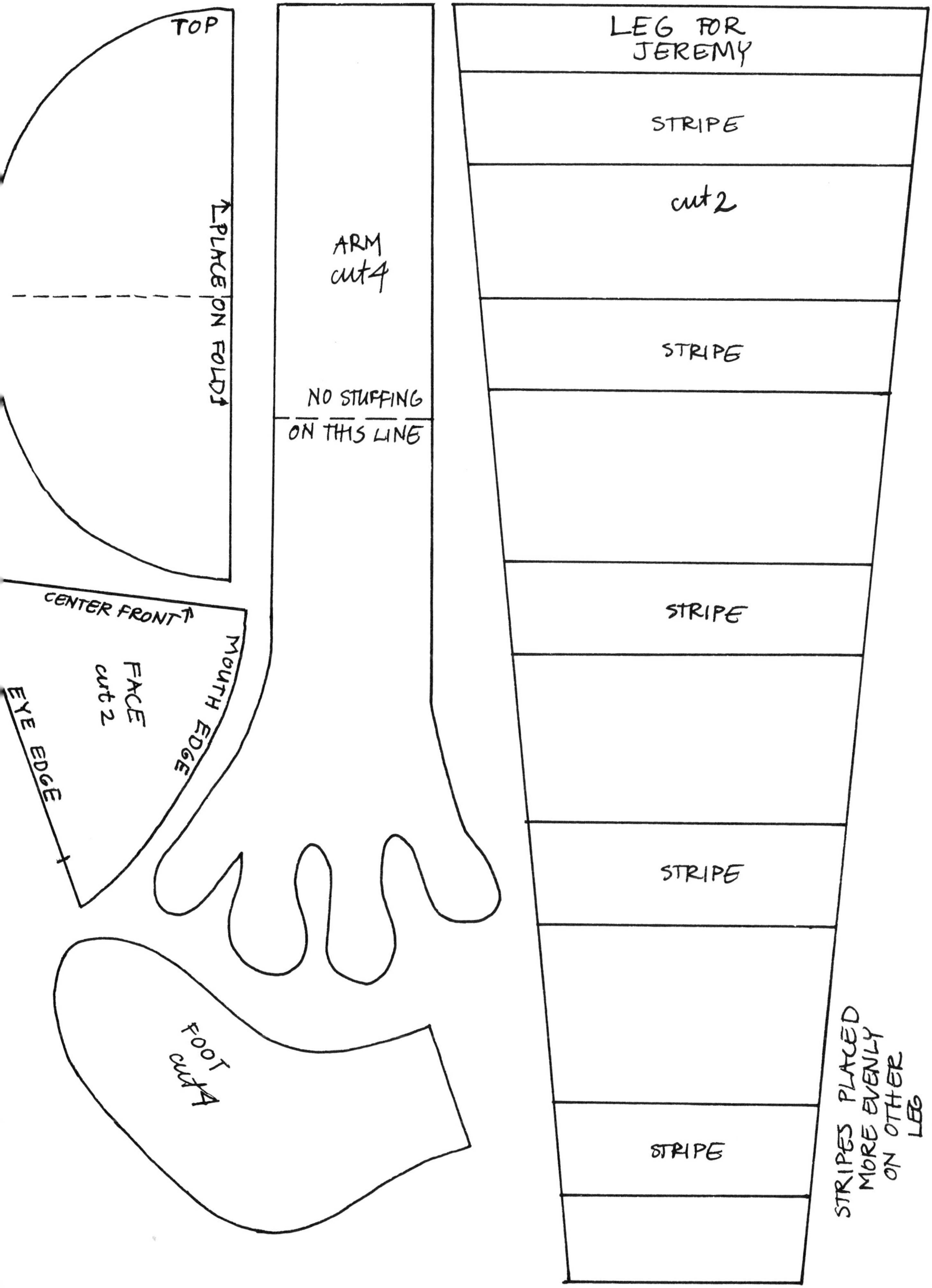

TOP

PLACE ON FOLD

CENTER FRONT

MOUTH EDGE

FACE
cut 2

EYE EDGE

FOOT
cut 4

ARM
cut 4

NO STUFFING
ON THIS LINE

LEG FOR
JEREMY

STRIPE

cut 2

STRIPE

STRIPE

STRIPE

STRIPE

STRIPE

STRIPES PLACED
MORE EVENLY
ON OTHER LEG

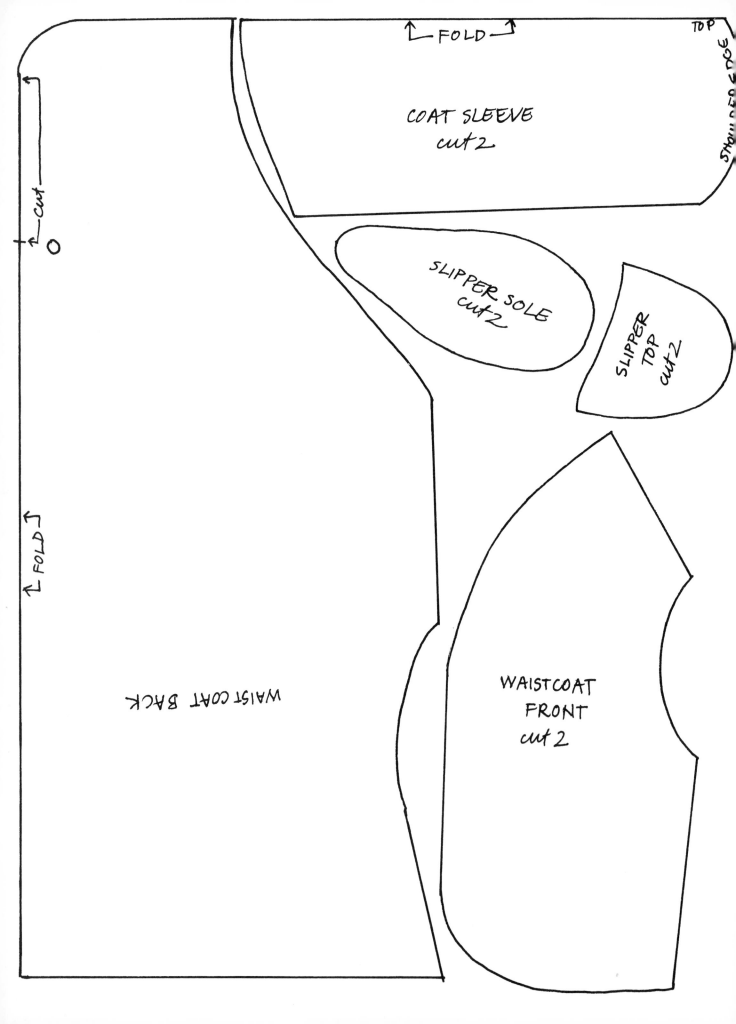

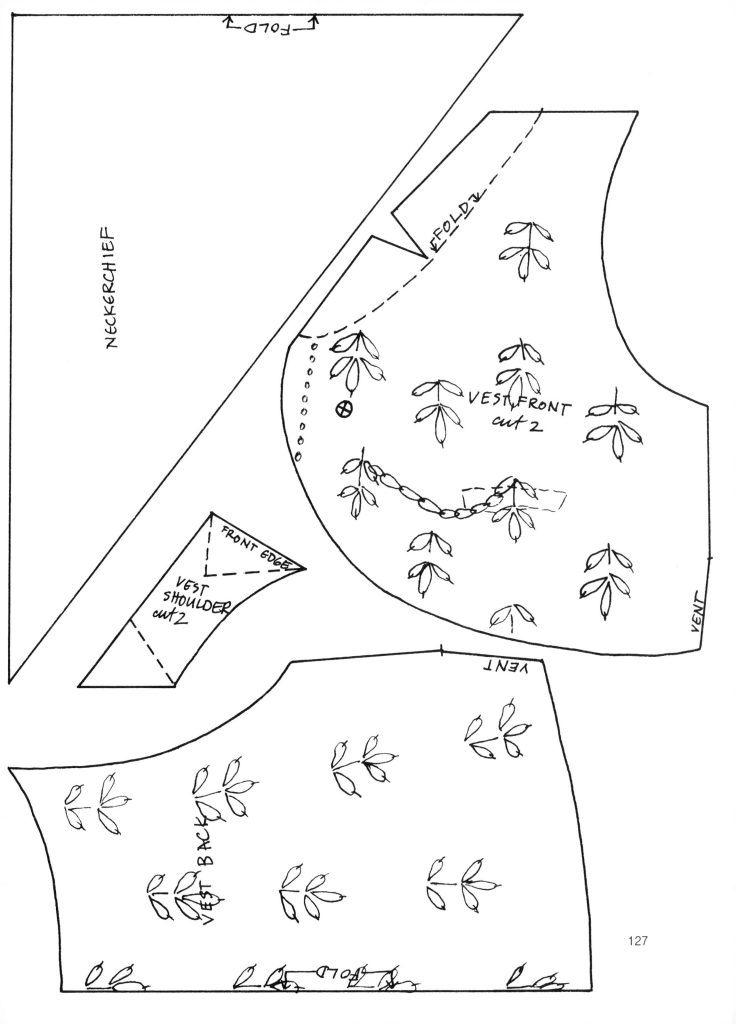

NECKERCHIEF

FOLD

FOLD

VEST FRONT
cut 2

VEST
SHOULDER
cut 2

FRONT EDGE

VENT

VENT

VEST BACK

FOLD

127

MOUSE, WORM, LADYBUG, AND OWL

A mouse, a ladybug, an owl and a worm are all extremely quick toys to make in cuddly latch-hooked yarn and certain to be friends with everybody. They'll come to life as you hook, then pad them, adding legs, whiskers, eyes, and ears in brightly colored felt.

MATERIALS

#5 Latch hook canvas
Latch hook
Precut rug yarn
Precut rya yarn
Uncut rug yarn
Felt
Loose batting

MOUSE

2 shades gray precut rya used together
Pale gray rug yarn for tail
Gray and pink felt for ears
Black and white precut rug yarn for eyes
White precut rug yarn for under tummy

ORDER OF WORKING

With a permanent marker, draw the outline of each animal on the canvas, counting from the graphs. Using the precut yarn, latch-hook as shown on page 159, starting with the top row and working down in horizontal rows. A quick and easy way to latch-hook is to hold 3 threads against the needle simultaneously, and latch them one by one into the canvas (see diagram).

SPECIAL DETAILS

WORM AND LADYBUG EYEBROWS. Cut a length of yarn 4″ long; latch 3 pieces together into 3 holes above eyes.

LADYBUG LEGS. Glue together (using clear white glue) two strips of black felt for stiffer legs.

LADYBUG EYES. Glue black circle to white and stitch firmly in place—to the canvas, not the surrounding wool.

MOUSE WHISKERS. Make a twisted cord as on page 38 and sew through after animal is complete.

MOUSE EARS. Cut felt ear shapes and glue smaller pink felt oval to larger gray ear. Attach firmly to canvas with heavy-duty thread.

MOUNTING

Using heavy-duty thread, hand-sew completed pieces together, right sides facing, carefully matching threads and holes of the canvas. Turn right sides out, stuff with batting, and sew up the opening. Attach ears, whiskers, etc., at this point.

The worm is too small to be joined in this way. The shapes should be cut out, turnbacks creased back, and the pieces overcast together.

ladybug

ladybug tummy

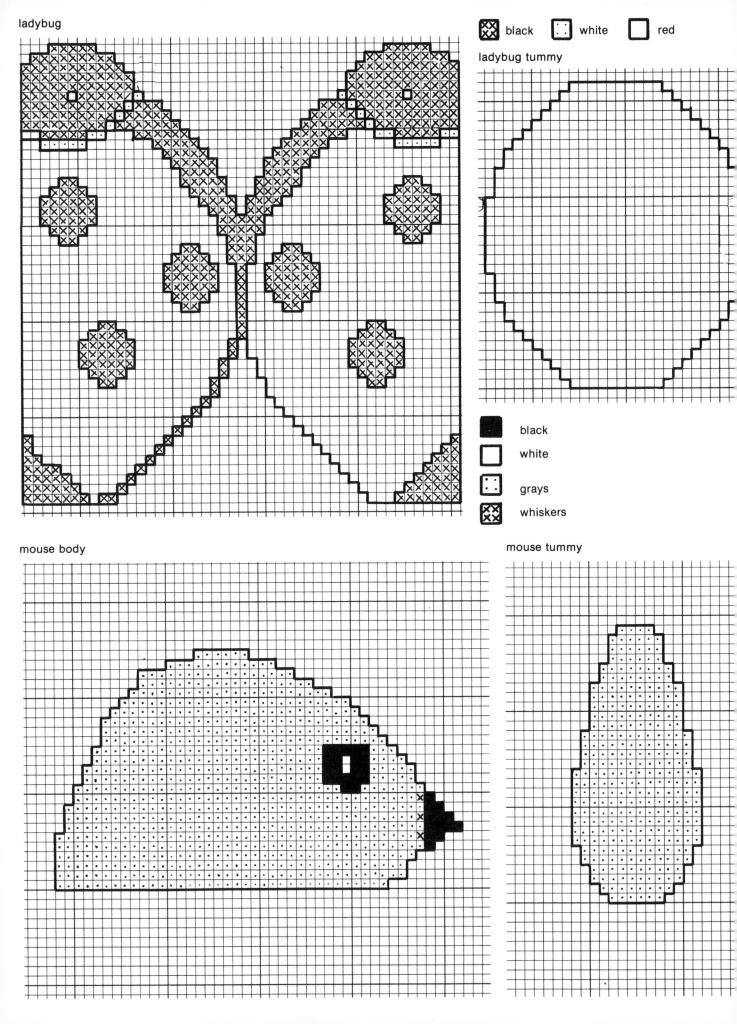

black

white

grays

whiskers

mouse body

mouse tummy

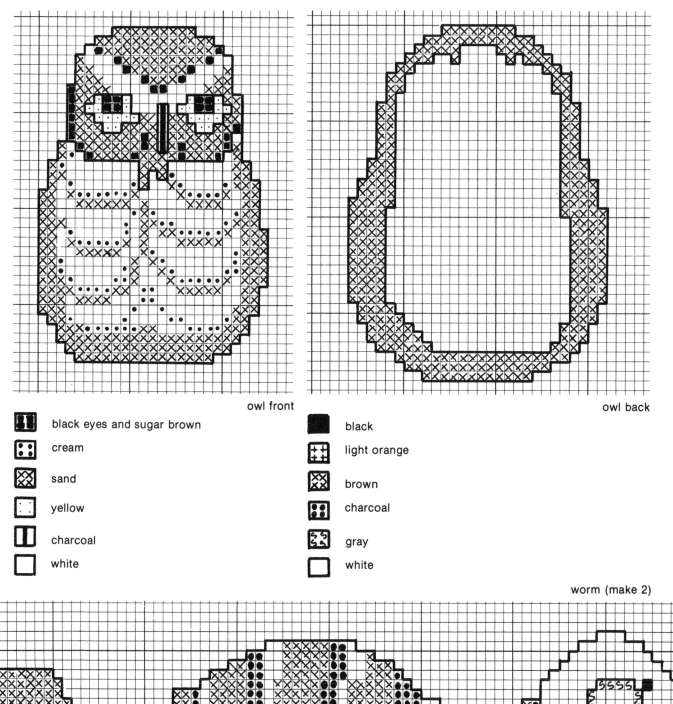

owl front

owl back

black eyes and sugar brown	black
cream	light orange
sand	brown
yellow	charcoal
charcoal	gray
white	white

worm (make 2)

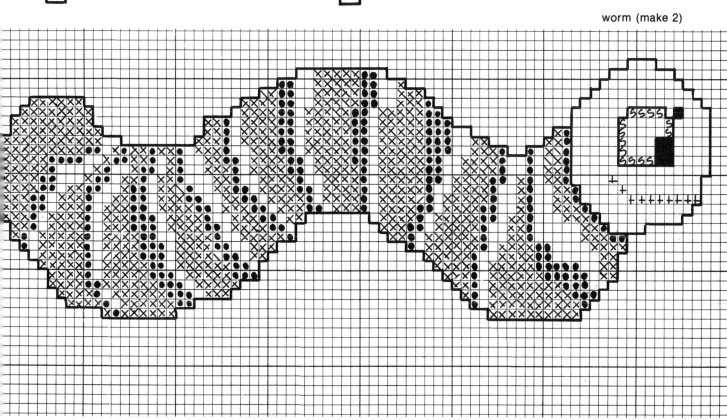

SANTA-IN-CHIMNEY PUPPET

Make a little felt box to represent the chimney, then make a finger puppet to represent Santa and pop him inside. This "toy" ornament for the tree is so quick and easy to make, it's a wonderful idea for a church bazaar—or it could be the very first ornament for a child to make (with just a little help in cutting out the shapes, perhaps).

MATERIALS

#7 plastic canvas
Nantuk acrylic yarn, brick red and beige
Craft glue
Sewing thread, red
Felt

ORDER OF WORKING

CHIMNEY

Cut 2 squares of plastic canvas 16 threads by 15 threads. Following diagram, work straight stitches in red to form bricks. Work rows of open buttonhole stitch (page 157) in between bricks as shown, then a row of close buttonholes along the top edge of both pieces. Whip-stitch (page 158) the 2 pieces together with red, leaving the top edges open to hold Santa.

SANTA

Trace the shapes on tissue paper from this page. Cut out the paper to use as a pattern for each section of Santa. Trace patterns on felt and cut out shapes. Sew base pieces together with whipping stitch, leaving lower edge open. Glue face together in layers—skin tone first, then mouth, beard, eyes, nose, and brim of hat, and, finally, add the white dot or a pompon (page 158).

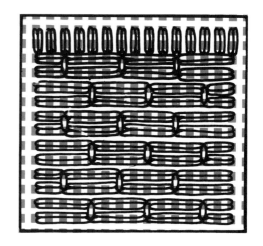

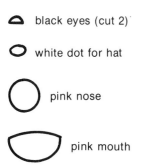

black eyes (cut 2)

white dot for hat

pink nose

pink mouth

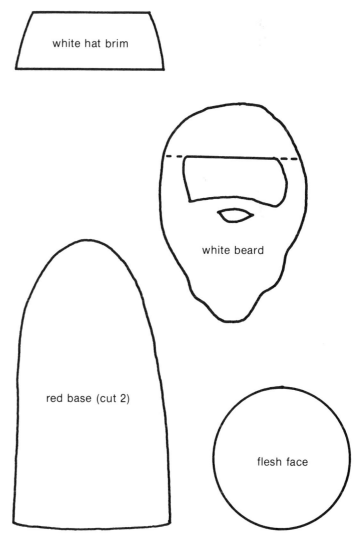

white hat brim

white beard

red base (cut 2)

flesh face

133

MINIATURE TOTE BAGS

Everyone's in love with miniatures, and here are some very small tote bags with Beatrix Potter's Peter Rabbit, Benjamin Bunny, and Squirrel Nutkin in needlepoint—just waiting to be filled with candies or tiny gifts. After Christmas they can be used in a sewing basket to hold a needle case, thimble, and cottons—and just think what a great little gift that could be for your sewing friends at Easter! So you can see how a little stitching can go a long way.

MATERIALS

Plastic canvas 10 to the inch, by the yard
Persian wool

ORDER OF WORKING

Count out the designs from the graph on plastic canvas. Work in needlepoint and add textured details, such as fluffy turkey-work tails, French-knot eyes, etc. Use the alphabet on pages 136–137 to initial the back of each bag. When complete, cut out each piece leaving one row of holes open around the needlepoint. Lace the worked pieces together with the whipping stitch shown on page 158, using a contrasting color. Line with a bright felt or cotton fabric.

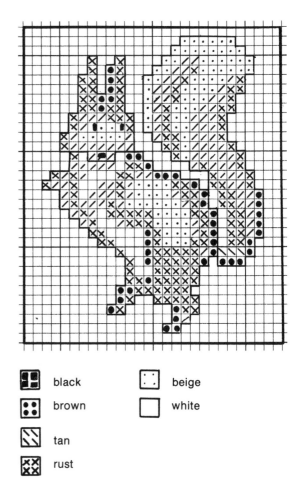

▦	black	⊡	beige
⊠	brown	☐	white
◩	tan		
▨	rust		

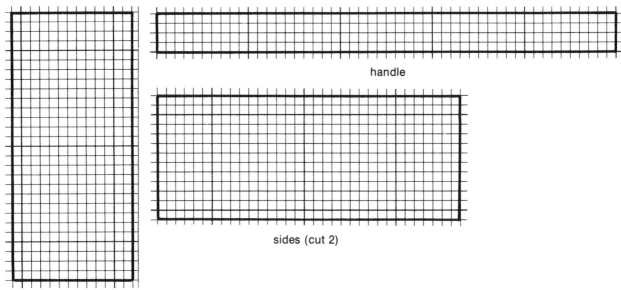

handle

sides (cut 2)

bottom

134

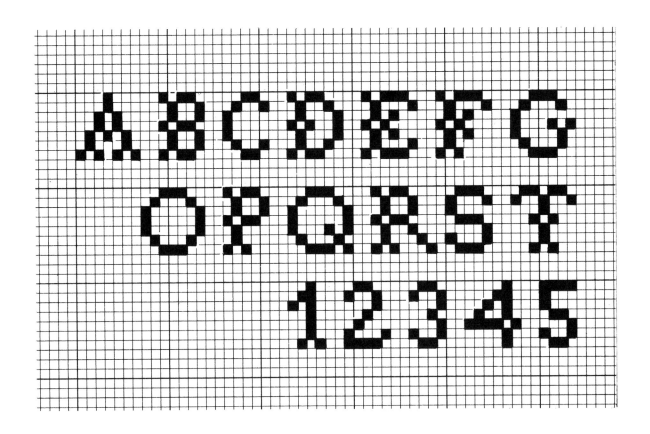

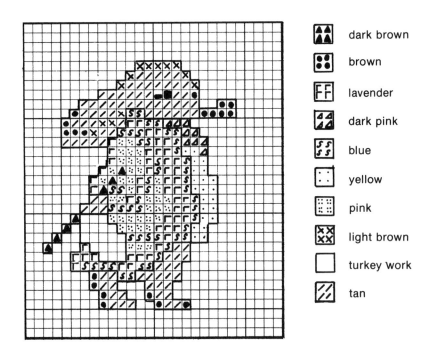

	dark brown
	brown
	lavender
	dark pink
	blue
	yellow
	pink
	light brown
	turkey work
	tan

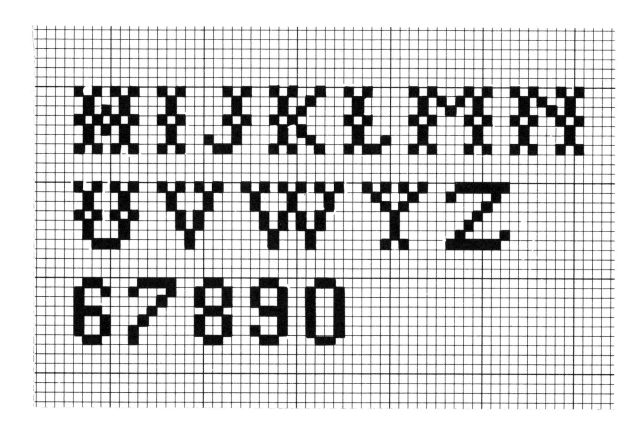

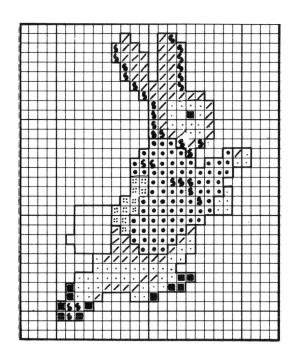

	turkey-work white
	tan
	light brown
	light blue
	dark blue
	brown
	black

SANTA IN A BALLOON

(Color Plate 4)

I can't think why Santa hasn't thought of arriving in a balloon before—it seems a much easier way to carry his sack and simply drop the presents down the chimney.

The balloon is made with quick, colorful stitches on #10 interlocked canvas in six sections. You can join the canvas afterward and pad it with Dacron batting or cover a Styrofoam ball. The basket is made in one strip, joined to make a round shape, and Santa is simply wrapped wool with a fluffy angora beard. In the scale shown here he will make a great Christmas mobile, but if you want to make him small enough to hang on the tree, simply work from the graph on #18 canvas.

MATERIALS

#10 interlocked canvas
Loose batting or styrofoam ball
Nantuk yarn
Angora yarn
Curtain rings
Contrasting felt or cotton lining for basket
Fishing line (monofilament) for hanging

ORDER OF WORKING

SANTA

Wrap red yarn around a piece of cardboard 4½" long to form a 1" thick clump. Insert a strand of yarn through the loops at the top edge and remove all yarn from cardboard. Pull strand tight to gather and knot. Form head by wrapping yarn 1½" below top. Divide yarn in half at bottom for legs. Make boots by first wrapping each foot with white angora yarn. Trace patterns on the next page and transfer to felt. Stitch boots and glue to each foot. Form arms by wrapping small amount of yarn around cardboard. Remove and tie 1" from either end to form hands. Insert arms through body and clip ends. Cut face and accessories from felt. Thread belt through the buckle and glue to body. Glue eyes to face. Gather a circle of red felt around edge and draw up tight to form a ball; add to face for bulb nose. Stitch hat, glue band around bottom, top with a pompon (page 158), and attach to head. Make

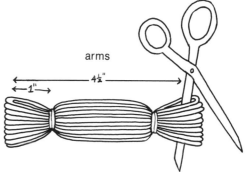

arms

139

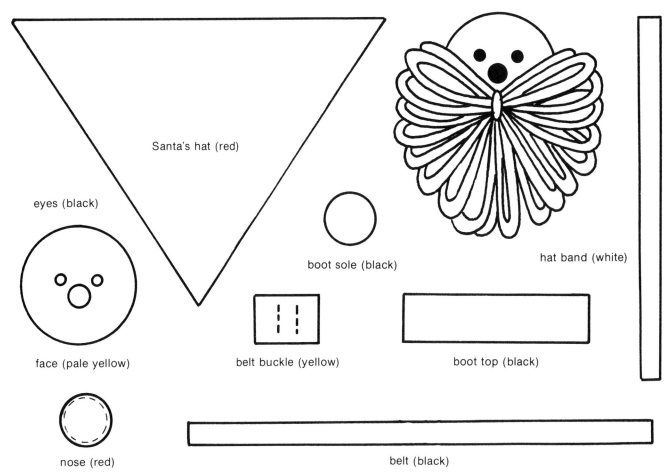

Santa's hat (red)

eyes (black)

boot sole (black)

hat band (white)

face (pale yellow)

belt buckle (yellow)

boot top (black)

nose (red)

belt (black)

beard by winding white angora yarn around fingers to form loops, tie in center, and glue to face.

BALLOON

You will be making 6 sections of canvas as shown on the graph on the next page. Only *half* of one section is shown so it could be actual size. Work each section in the following way: With a hard (H) pencil, mark a vertical line 12" long, and draw a horizontal line 4 inches wide through the center (shown by broken lines). Leave at least 1½" for seam allowance on the canvas all around. Starting on the center line and using 1 thread of knitting-weight wool, fill each section with long vertical stitches, as shown on the graph. Follow the color scheme of red, blue, yellow, and white shown in Color Plate 4 or use your own. Work the basket in the same way to form a strip 3½" x 11" and a circle 3½" in diameter. When all 6 sections of the balloon are worked, block them and trim, leaving a ½" seam allowance. Join by taking 2 sections with right sides facing, line up the pattern, and seam by

hand or machine. Continue attaching sections until all 6 pieces are joined. To complete the ball, stuff with batting and blind-stitch the last seam together. Cut a circle of felt for the base of the basket, and cut a piece of felt 3½" x 11" to line the basket. With an overcast stitch, sew the brass rings to the center of each seam around the "equator" of the ball.

Cut 2 pieces of yarn 80" long and twist into a 20" cord (see page 28). Make 6 and pull through the brass ring and basket, as shown in the photo. To hang the balloon, tie a 15" piece of monofilament to each ring, and attach them all to a brass ring on top of the balloon.

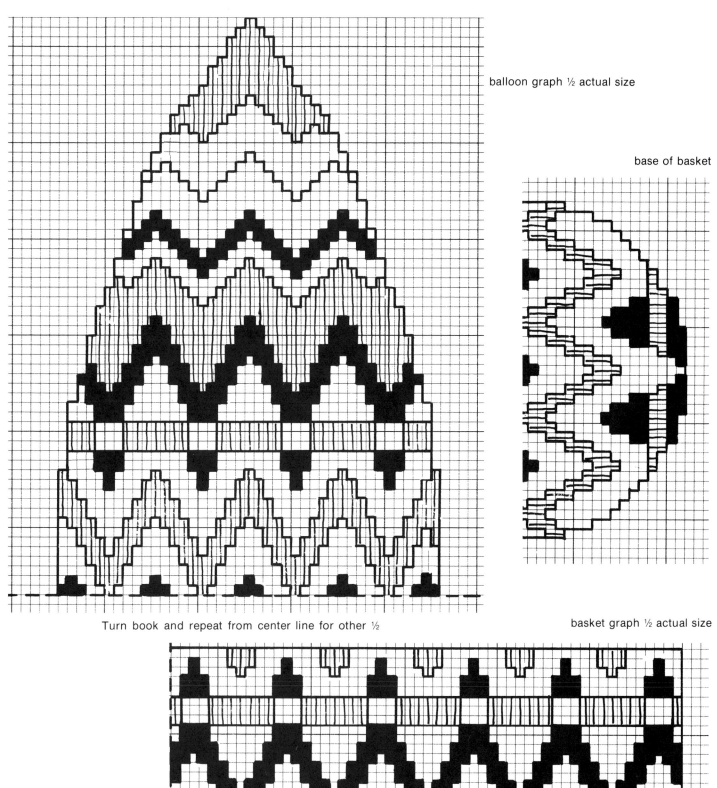

balloon graph ½ actual size

base of basket

Turn book and repeat from center line for other ½

basket graph ½ actual size

center line

Repeat from center line for other ½

"I'M A CHRISTMAS ANGEL"

A quickly stitched cross-stitch bib will make you the most popular granny or mum in the world—and certainly the youngest member of the household should not be forgotten at Christmas!

MATERIALS

Prequilted cotton/polyester fabric
Prefolded seam binding
Cotton embroidery floss
#10 waste canvas

ORDER OF WORKING

Outline a simple bib shape onto prequilted fabric. Stretch it in a hoop and baste a piece of waste canvas on top. Using the canvas as a grid, count out the design from the graph shown here, working in cross stitch over 1 cross thread of the canvas. Use 2 strands of embroidery floss throughout. When all the stitching is complete, draw out the waste canvas, thread by thread, leaving the cross stitches on the fabric (see diagrams on page 144). Wetting the canvas will soften it and make it easier to pull out. Add backstitch outlines as shown in the graph. Now, repeat the process to work the cloud-shaped pocket shown on page 145. Cut out the bib and pocket and cover the raw edges with seam binding. Leave the seam binding long at the top, for ties. Sew blue seam binding around the pocket, and appliqué the pocket onto the bib, leaving it open at the top.

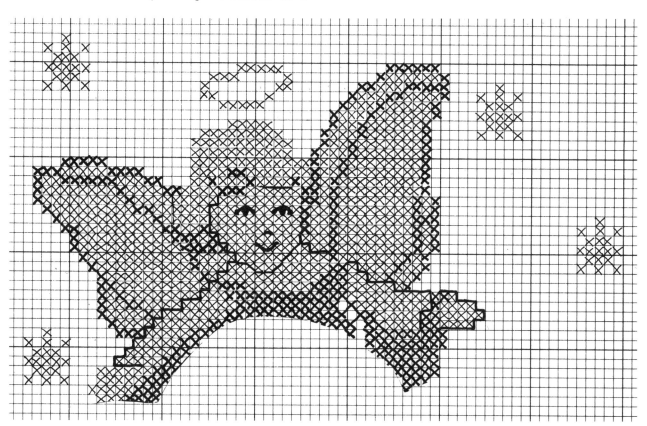

COLOR CHART. Work the halo and stars in medium yellow; the hair in light yellow with shadows of gold; the face and hands in flesh, outlined in medium pink. The dress is worked at the top in light pink, shading into medium pink at the sleeve edges and dark pink at the bottom and for the outline. The wings are light blue in the central areas, surrounded by white and edged in medium blue. The eyes and lettering are blue; the mouth and nose medium pink.

Erica's daughter Vanessa with "a Christmas angel."

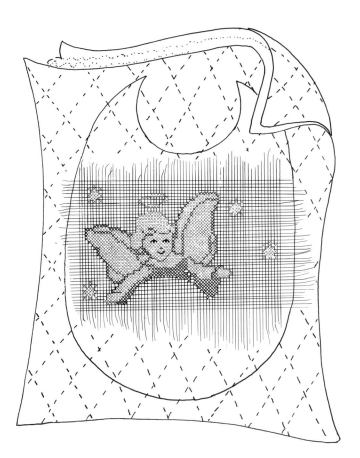

Opposite page: Pocket is stitched along sides and base. The top is left open (between asterisks *) to form the pocket.

1. Waste canvas on prequilted fabric with angel completed in cross stitch, counted from graph on previous page.

2. Canvas threads being drawn out, leaving cross-stitch angel ready for pocket to be stitched in place below.

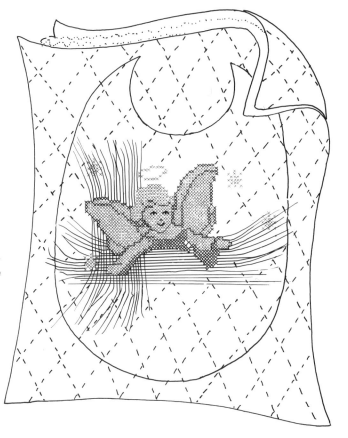

I'm
a Christmas
Angel

THE OWL FAMILY

A Christmas tree that looks as though you just carried it in from the woods with the animals still attached can be a delightfully different approach. All-wool "creatures" give it an old-fashioned country atmosphere and by adding just a few little white lights can give it a frosty sparkle. The stitch is turkey work, a series of loops that give you a furry velvet effect when clipped. You might start with owls, then continue on to squirrels, chipmunks, or raccoons to create a tree full of your favorite birds and animals.

MATERIALS

Linen or cotton homespun fabric
Persian wool, 3 strands
Dacron batting

ORDER OF WORKING

Trace patterns on pages 148–149 to fabric (see page 154 for method).

Begin with the eyes. Using 1 strand of Persian wool, work the pupil in black satin stitch and the iris in yellow satin stitch. Then outline the top of the eye in gray, and the bottom of the eye in black, stem stitch. Work the beak in a single black bullion knot.

Using all 3 strands, work the owl's body in rows of turkey work; loops should be about 1¼" long. Each line represents the stitch direction and color. The circled areas above the eyes indicate the owl's horns. Work them longer than the rest.

When all stitching is complete, cut out each piece leaving a ½" seam allowance. With right sides facing, sew the front and back together leaving an opening for stuffing. Turn right side out, stuff, and slip-stitch closed.

The owls come to life with the trimming. Begin around the eyes and nose, cutting the loops right around the eyes to about ¼". As you move out toward the crown, trim to about ¾". Leave the horns at about 1¼". Trim the body to about 1". As you cut, comb through the wool with your fingers. This will blend the colors and allow you to see how the "haircut" is progressing.

Loop an 8" strand of yarn at the top of the head for hanging on the tree.

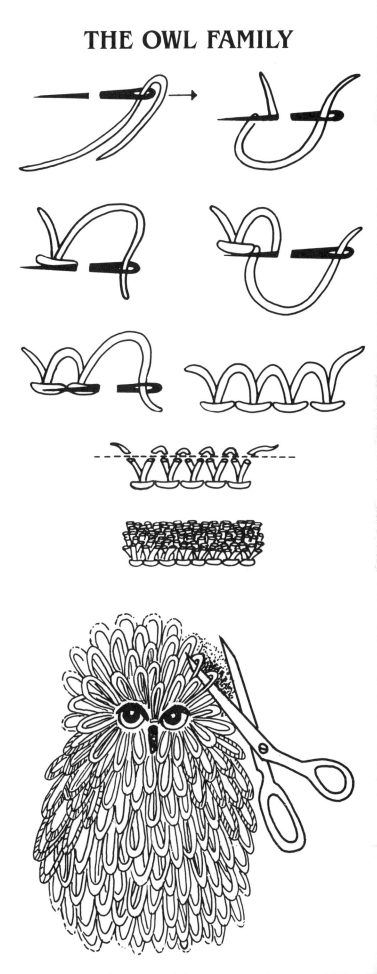

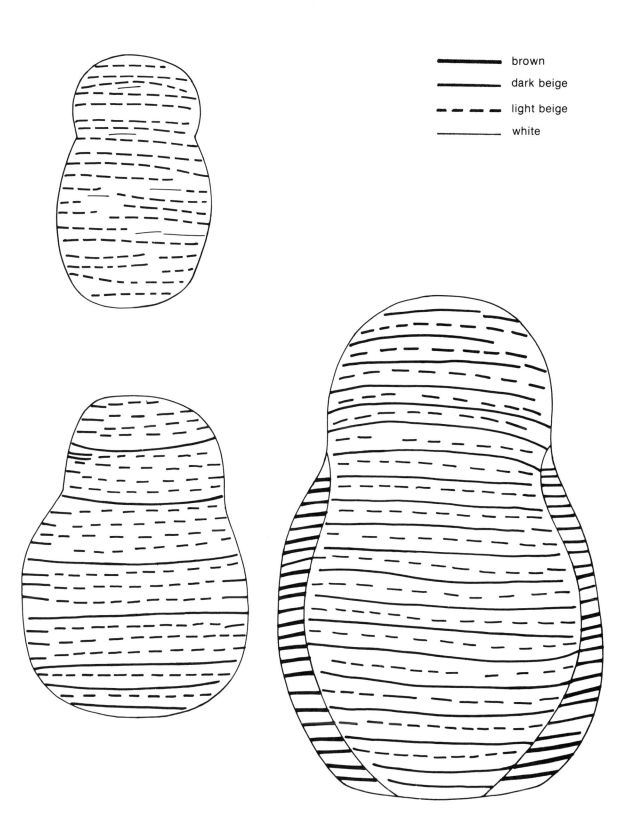

brown
dark beige
light beige
white

GONE TO BED—OWL DOOR PILLOW

Here is the pillow to hang on your bedroom door when all the presents have been unwrapped and Christmas Day is over. The fluffy owl is worked in the same way as the ornaments on page 146 and popped into the mossy nest appliquéd in 3-D in that ideal "nest" stitch, the crazy cross-stitch. And when all is said and done, you can close your door and realize there are only 364 days left before Christmas.

MATERIALS

Medium weight cotton cottage cloth, a
   homespun fabric—oyster
Persian wool
Felt, velvet, or similar fabric for backing

ORDER OF WORKING

(1) Trace the design according to instructions on page 154. The finished door pillow measures 5" x 7". The top of the nest is worked separately and appliquéd on later, so be sure to leave plenty of fabric between pieces. (2) Work branches in long and short stitch vertically, blending dark beige and dark khaki brown. (3) Work the leaves in fishbone stitch (page 156), the two at the bottom right in light green, the remaining in dark leaf green. (4) Work the lettering in backstitch in dark leaf green. (5) Work the back of the nest in crazy cross-stitch in dark leaf green, light khaki brown, dark khaki brown, light leaf green, olive green, and gold. Beginning with the first color listed, stitches should be worked fairly large and at random. The colors are blended by overlapping the stitches, starting with the darker color at top and shading to the lightest at the sides and bottom of the nest. (6) Work the top of the nest in the same fashion in light leaf green, olive green, light khaki brown, dark leaf green, light khaki brown, dark leaf green, and gold. Blend the colors in the order listed, from the top of the nest to the sides and bottom. When all stitching is completed, cut it out, hem over the folds, curve to form a pocket, and appliqué to the back of the nest. (7) Work the owl in the same way as the smallest owl on page 146. (8) Complete the door sign as described on page 106 and sleep tight.

Crazy cross-stitch

150

Gone to bed

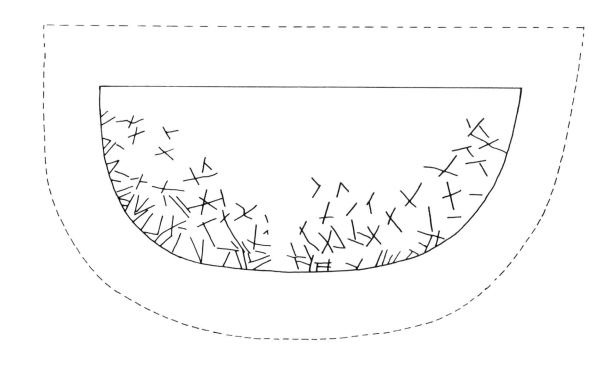

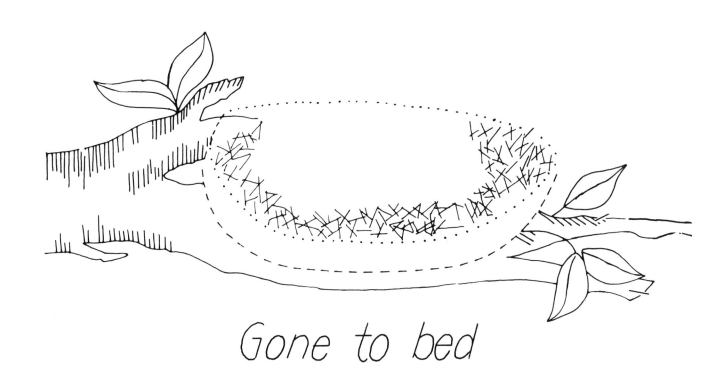

Gone to bed

USING THE DESIGNS IN THIS BOOK

WORKING WITH A FRAME

Most needlework is easier and better worked if the background fabric is stretched taut. The fabric must be stretched really tight in order to keep the stitches even, and an embroidery frame will allow you to do this. The best type of hoop frame has a stand or support that allows you to work with both hands free—one above and one below the frame. In this way you can work quickly and smoothly with an even rhythm.

Left to right: Standing floor frame with 12-inch hoop; 36-inch oval rug frame; stretcher strip frame (available in ½-inch modules); lap or Fanny® frame with 10-inch hoop. (Hoops and bases of the "fanny" and floor frames are interchangeable.)

ENLARGING OR REDUCING DESIGNS

Most of the designs in this book are drawn life-size so that you can trace them right from the book. Should you need to enlarge or reduce any designs, the best method is probably the use of a photostat. Photostat services are available in most towns (available through the Yellow Pages under "Photocopying" or "Blueprint"). Only one measurement need be given—height or width —for the designs to be enlarged proportionately, and you will be ready to trace it in exactly the size you require.

Another method is to enlarge or reduce the design from a graph created over it. Draw equally spaced horizontal and vertical lines over the design surface, forming a grid of square boxes. On a separate sheet of paper, draw an equal number of *larger* (or *smaller*) boxes, which will make up the desired size (square or rectangle) of your finished design. Transfer the original design, box by box, to the new sheet. You'll find that even the most complicated design can be redrawn quite easily when reduced to a few lines within a small box.

TRANSFERRING THE DESIGNS

Always use the same basic procedure when preparing fabric for design transferring. Fold the material in half vertically right down the center and repeat this horizontally. Mark these crease lines by running a hard pencil lightly between the threads of canvas, or by basting lines on fabric. Repeat this on your paper pattern; then, while you lay one on top of the other, align the lines to keep the design centered and square. Edge your fabric with masking tape, or hem, or oversew it all around to prevent fraying while the work is in progress.

TRANSFERRING TO FABRIC

Three excellent methods of transferring your crewel designs to fabric are tracing, dressmaker's carbon paper, and fusible web.

TRACING

You can trace your design directly to the fabric with a washable marker (my own brand of pens is called Trace-Erase, because you can "erase" the blue lines by simply dabbing them with cold water). Sheer materials, such as organdy, allow you to see the design through the fabric, making transferring easy with a hard "H" pencil or a Trace-Erase marker. Not-so-sheer fabrics, such as cottons and linens, might require back lighting to make the design visible beneath the fabric.

CARBON PAPER

Another method of transferring to fabric is with dressmaker's carbon (ordinary carbon paper will smudge). Use blue carbon for light-color fabrics, white for dark ones. Tape your fabric down on all four sides to a smooth hard surface and place your design on top. Now slide a sheet of carbon paper face downward between the paper and material. Anchor the design with some heavy books and trace, pressing firmly with a pencil. You can lift a corner occasionally to see how well your design is transferring.

FUSIBLE WEB

Fusible web (Stitch Witchery and Wonder Under are two brands) is an excellent method for transferring your design to all types of fabrics—especially fabrics in dark colors or with pile. Choose the lightest weight (and most transparent) fusible web and place it over your design. Trace your design onto the web and baste the web in position on your fabric. Stitch directly onto the fabric, through the web. When your crewel piece is complete, the web can be torn away, leaving only your stitches.

TRANSFERRING TO CANVAS

Designs for needlepoint can be transferred to canvas by following graphs or by tracing with a permanent marker. Designs on plastic canvas are best worked from graphs. Always work on a square (or rectangular) piece of fabric—cut it to shape after the needlework is finished, and always allow plenty of extra fabric for mounting and blocking.

TRACING

Tracing is the best method for transferring a design to needlepoint canvas. To begin, draw your design on paper with India ink or with a black waterproof felt-tipped pen. Lay it on a table or firm surface, and hold it in position with masking tape. Establish the center of the canvas and design, and trace the design on the canvas, using a black waterproof felt-tipped pen or a fine paintbrush and India ink. (Test the pen to make sure the ink will not run when the canvas is blocked.) Then draw the design with a fine light line—a heavy black line may be hard to cover with light-colored wools. Draw the design as you would on paper, making the lines smooth and flowing (not a series of steps following the square mesh).

GRAPHS

Geometric designs do not have to be applied; they are counted directly from a graph onto the plain canvas or evenweave fabric. Always begin in the middle and work out to the edges, so that your repeat pattern will be balanced and identical on both sides. Always count the threads of the canvas, never the holes. This makes it much less confusing when you are deciding on the size of each stitch and means your counting will be consistent. One square of the graph represents one stitch on the canvas. To mark the edges of the design, it is not necessary to rule the lines; simply draw the pencil between the threads of the canvas in the same way you marked the center.

BEGINNING AND ENDING CREWEL AND ANY COMBINATION OF CREWEL STITCHES ON PLASTIC CANVAS

On fabric, start with a knot on the reverse side, and end with two tiny backstitches on a nearby outline. These will lock the thread in place and will be covered by the subsequent stitching. Follow the same procedure for plastic canvas, but for strength and security, use the backstitches for both beginning *and* ending, placing them in the *center* of the shape, where they will be completely hidden by stitching.

BEGINNING AND ENDING NEEDLEPOINT

Knot the thread and take the needle down through the front of the canvas a short distance from where you want to begin (about 6 threads away). Work toward the knot, covering the long thread on the reverse side. When the thread is locked in by your stitches, cut off the knot—the thread will be held securely in place by your close stitching. End off in the same way.

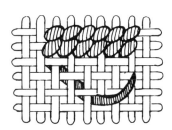

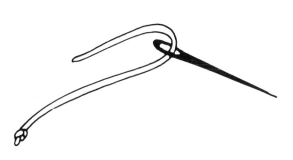

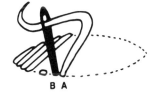

B A

STITCH DICTIONARY

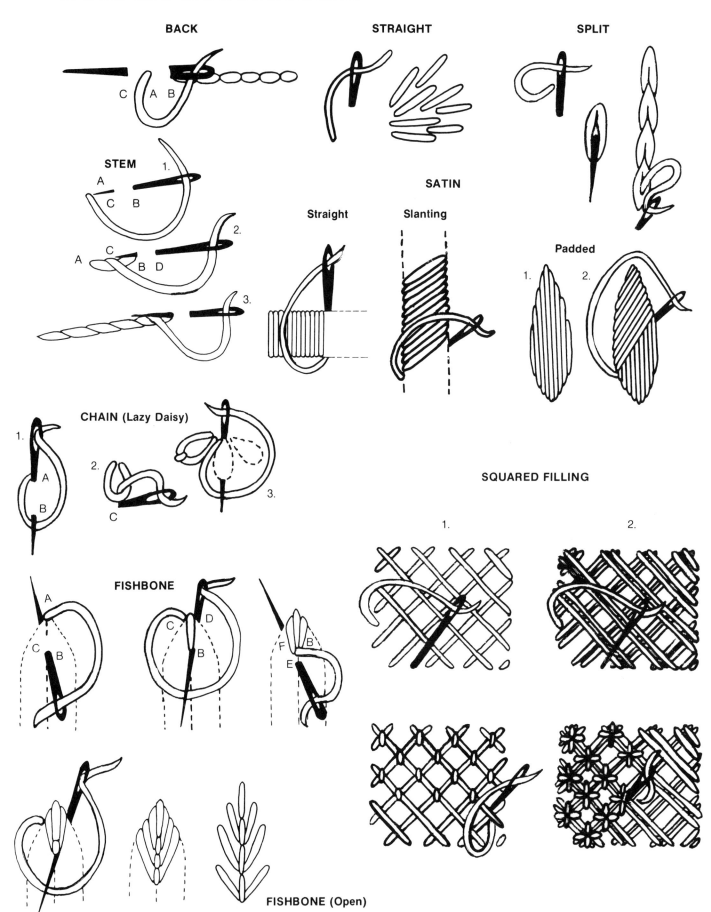

BACK

STRAIGHT

SPLIT

STEM

SATIN

Straight

Slanting

Padded

CHAIN (Lazy Daisy)

SQUARED FILLING

1.

2.

FISHBONE

FISHBONE (Open)

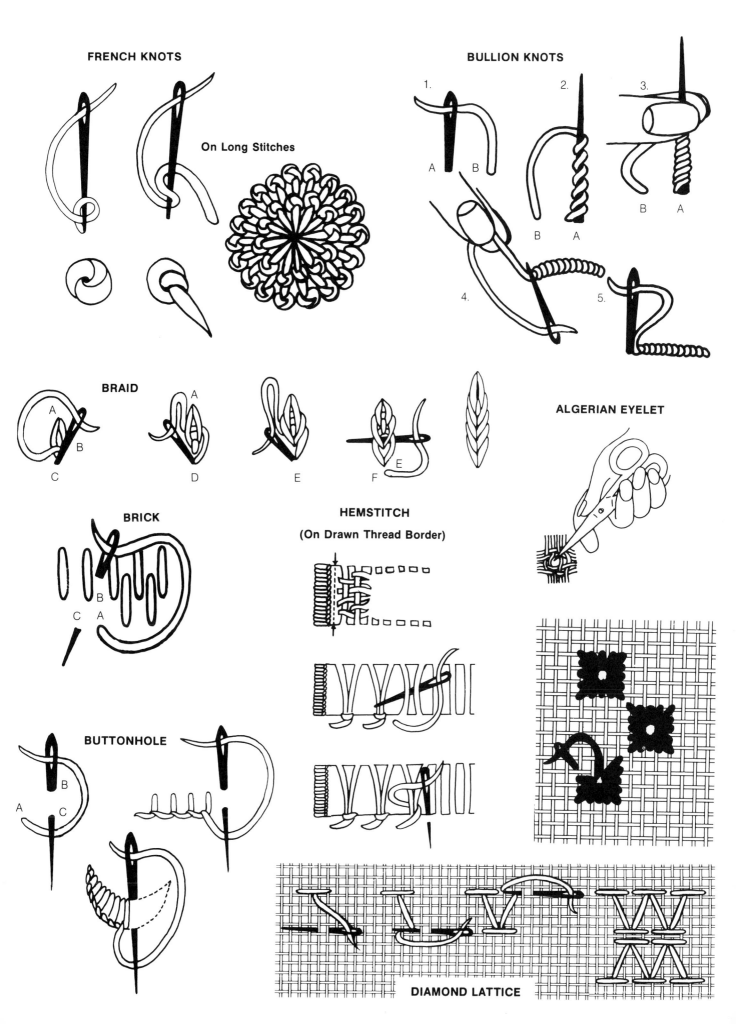

FRENCH KNOTS

On Long Stitches

BULLION KNOTS

1.
A   B

2.
B   A

3.
B   A

4.

5.

BRAID

A
B
C

A
D

E

F
E

ALGERIAN EYELET

BRICK

B
C   A

HEMSTITCH

(On Drawn Thread Border)

BUTTONHOLE

A
B
C

DIAMOND LATTICE

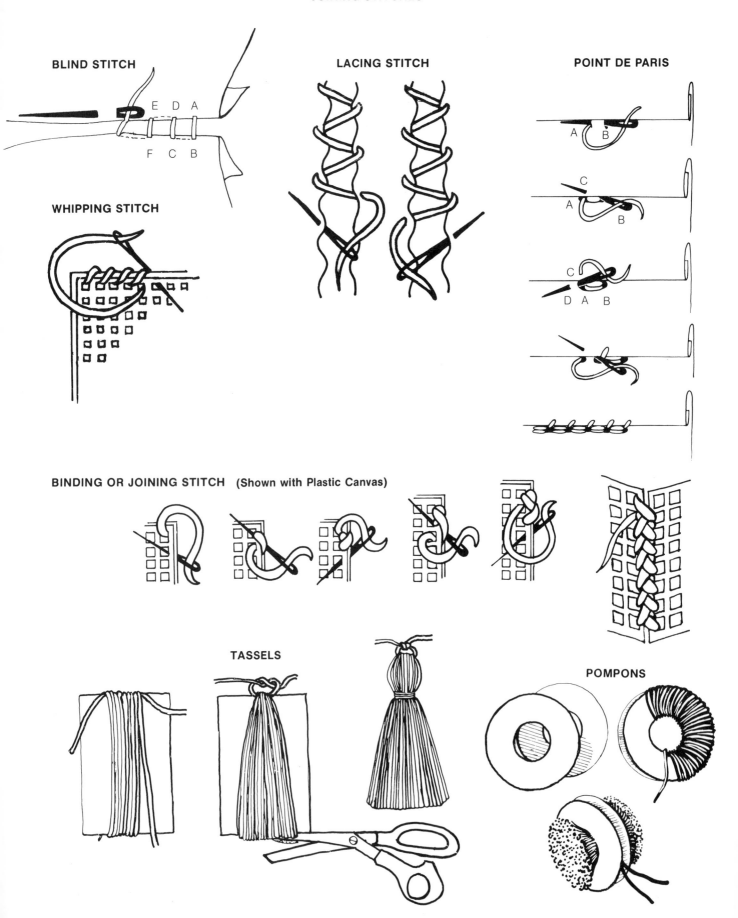

JOINING STITCHES

BLIND STITCH

E D A

F C B

WHIPPING STITCH

LACING STITCH

POINT DE PARIS

A B

C
A B

C
D A B

BINDING OR JOINING STITCH (Shown with Plastic Canvas)

TASSELS

POMPONS

QUILTING

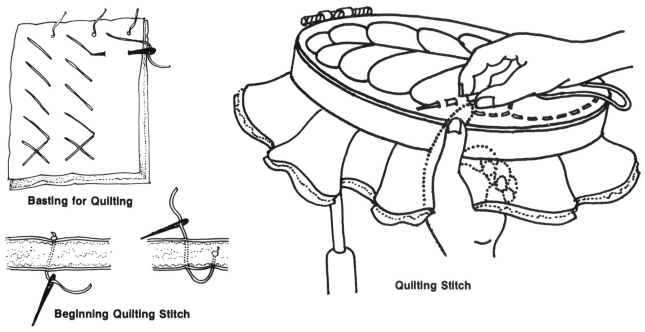

Basting for Quilting

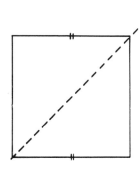

Beginning Quilting Stitch

Quilting Stitch

LATCH HOOKING

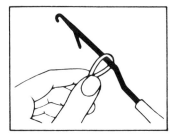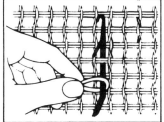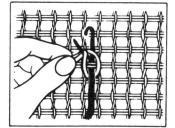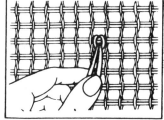

CUTTING CONTINUOUS BIAS

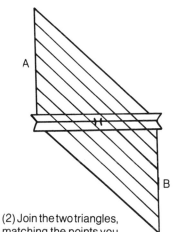

(1) On a large square of fabric (1 yard, 36 inches wide, for instance), mark the center of the width on each side. Cut the fabric in half diagonally, as shown.

(2) Join the two triangles, matching the points you marked before cutting. Using tailor's chalk, rule parallel lines across the longest length at approximately 2- to 4-inch intervals (depending on the width you want the binding to be), as shown.

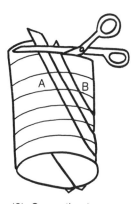

(3) Seam the two opposite sides (A & B) together to form a sleeve, as shown. Make sure one edge projects above the other at the seam by one width, as shown, and that the other markings match and run straight across the seam. Also make sure that the raw edges of both the first seam and the sleeve seam are on the same side.

(4) Proceed to cut around along the chalked lines to form one continuous bias strip (rather like peeling an apple).

SUPPLIERS

Aida cloth: Joan Toggitt Ltd.
Appleton wool: Erica Wilson Needleworks
Batting ("Mountain Mist"): Stearns & Foster Co.
Braids (silver and gold): La Lamé
Camelot gold and silver yarn: Columbia-
   Minerva, Erica Wilson Needleworks
Canvas by-the-yard: Joan Toggitt Ltd.
Cords (silver and gold): La Lamé
Danish flower thread: Erica Wilson Needleworks
Embroidery frames: Erica Wilson Needleworks
Fabrics, embroidery: Joan Toggitt Ltd.
FashionEase plastic canvas (sheets, squares,
   diamonds, by-the-yard): Columbia-Minerva
Fil d'argent (silver thread): DMC, Erica Wilson
   Needleworks
Fil d'or (gold thread): DMC, Erica Wilson
   Needleworks
Japanese gold thread: Erica Wilson
   Needleworks
Liquid embroidery (for painting on cloth):
   Tri-Chem Co.
Lurex threads: La Lamé
Maltese (horsetail) silk: Erica Wilson
   Needleworks
Metal threads: Erica Wilson Needleworks
Nantuk acrylic 4-ply yarn: Columbia-Minerva
Pentel wax crayons: Arthur Brown Art Supply
Waste canvas: Joan Toggitt Ltd.

Arthur Brown Art Supply
2 West 46th Street
New York, N.Y. 10036

Columbia-Minerva Corp.
Consumer Service
P. O. Box 500
Robesonia, Pa. 19551

DMC
107 Trumbull Street
Elizabeth, N.J. 07206

La Lamé
1170 Broadway
New York, N.Y. 10001

Stearns & Foster Co.
Cincinnati, Ohio 45215

Joan Toggitt Ltd.
246 Fifth Avenue
New York, N.Y. 10001

Tri-Chem Co.
Belleville, N.J. 07109

Erica Wilson Needleworks
717 Madison Avenue
New York, N.Y. 10021